Awake
Great Britain!

Awake Great Britain!

Wale Babatunde

Xpression Books

Xpression books is an imprint of

New Wine Ministries
PO Box 17
Chichester
West Sussex
United Kingdom
PO20 6YB

ISBN 1 903725 47 X

Typeset by CRB Associates, Reepham, Norfolk
Cover design by CCD, www.ccdgroup.co.uk
Printed in Malta

Dedication

*This book is dedicated to my wife Precious and
my three wonderful children Joshua, Grace and Jeremiah.
It is my prayer that you will be mighty arrows
in the hand of the Lord!*

Contents

Endorsements

Pastor Wale has hit upon some critical issues of the Church, not just relevant for Britain, but for many other nations as well. His genuine heart for kingdom impact is obvious and his plea for action is rooted in love and blessing. His cry for the Church to rise up in this hour is a clarion call that should not be ignored!
Rev. Murray Dodds, Director, Canadian Institute for Global Affairs

This book will challenge your political correctness and motivate you to believe again that, as we position ourselves correctly, God will hear our cry for our nation. Now is **not** a good time to be sleeping but we must arise and take our responsibility for this land. This book will stimulate and instruct you to respond to this cry.
Rachel Hickson, Founder and Director of Heartcry Ministries and Founder of the M25 London Prayernet. Rachel is married to Gordon, who is Associate Minister St Aldate's Church, Oxford

I heartily recommend this book. It makes the British public and the Church in general aware of highly dangerous trends in our society. It is a timely wake-up call.
Wynne Lewis, Senior Pastor, Kensington Temple (1980–1991), General Superintendent, Elim Churches (1991–2000)

A man's passion and purpose is many a time reflected in his writing. Pastor Wale's book reveals his heart; a desire to see reform at every level of society. God please give us many more men and women with this kind of fire and fervour!
Dr Jonathan Oloyede, Borough Dean Newham, Senior Associate Pastor Glory House, Team Leader Soul in the City

Pastor Wale writes with the passion of a man who sees a nation move relentlessly towards a precipice. This book is truly a wake-up call, rooted in Scripture and historical research, but one that also calls for corresponding practical action. Read the book prayerfully, come to your own conclusions as to the right way forward, but as you read I am sure you will experience an awakening.

Martin Scott, *author of* Gaining Ground *and* Impacting the City, *Prayer Leader and prophetic ministry, Sowing Seeds for Revival.*

The Heritage of Christian influences in Great Britain has provided the framework for freedoms enjoyed by all religions today. Christians hold firmly to the human right of any person to worship according to the dictates of his or her conscience. We also believe in the free exchange of ideas and liberty to share the Good News of Jesus Christ with everyone. This sets the Christian faith in dazzling juxtaposition to religious ideologies that incite intolerance and violence. Yet some beneficiaries of the very liberty the Gospel produces now wish to silence its source. The erosion of biblical values and their benefits to any society calls for today's followers of Jesus to be potent salt and brilliant light. While many today are producing an uncertain sound, Wale Babatunde issues a clear call for today's believers to display the Gospel of Jesus Christ in truth and love.

David Shibley, *President, Global Advance, Dallas, Texas, USA*

To read Pastor Wale's account of things in Great Britain and to rise to responsible action are all one and the same thing.

Bishop Robert E. Smith, SR, *Total Outreach for Christ Ministries, Little Rock, Arkansas, USA*

Wale Babatunde's book is a wise and desperately needed wake-up call to the Church to understand the grave crisis facing Britain and urgently respond to it in the way God wants us to. With the escalating de-Christianisation of British society, a conflict is raging for the soul of the nation. The relentless attacks on Britain's Christian heritage are unprecedented yet much of the British Church remains fast asleep and time is running out. As Britain moves ever more quickly towards divine judgment, I hope and pray that many British Christians will seriously take heed of Wale's urgent message.

Wilfred Wong, *Editorial Board Member,* Prophecy Today *Magazine*

This book should be read by every Christian in the land. It is written by a man who is widely respected for his deep faith and his commitment to the Kingdom of God. My dear friend, Wale Babatunde, has undoubtedly been prompted by God to make a mighty prophetic call to the churches in the United Kingdom. He has seen with very clear eyes what is happening in our land. He gives clear evidence of a nation and Church in crisis. He has shared the sadness of God as he sees the nation turning its back on Him and also sees the widespread apathy, confusion and unbelief amongst His people. Some of his interpretations will undoubtedly generate opposition, but that is part of the role of being a prophet. This book is provocative and challenging and is rooted in the raw Gospel. I pray that the Lord will use it to break down the barriers of indifference which besiege the Church and to arouse God's people from their slumber.

Dennis Wrigley, *The Maranatha Community, Manchester*

The Lord gave me the desire to host gatherings called "Awaken", and Wale was the first person on my heart to invite to speak. This powerful book gives a 'wake-up' call to the Body of Christ and helps you learn how to pray with understanding, without losing heart, or falling asleep. It gives fresh insight from the Holy Spirit into the oneness believers are being drawn into, and as you read it and join the growing Body of Christ who are worshipping and interceding in prayer for the nation, you will be blessed.

Julie Anderson, *Prayer for the Nations*

Acknowledgments

I am greatly indebted to many people.

Tolu, my administrative assistant, did the bulk of the typing; Sam Solomon, for your counsel and editorial assistance. To all my prayer partners around the world, who daily intercede on my behalf; to all my friends, partners in ministry, sons and daughters in World Harvest, you know who you are. You have not only ministered to me again and again, but you often refreshed and released me to fulfil my divine assignment.

To my parents, for the Christian heritage I received from you.

To Julie Anderson my wonderful friend through whose kind invitation God birthed this book. May God reward you here on earth and in the world to come. I love and appreciate you dearly.

Foreword

On my recent visits to England my spirit was grieved beyond words by the spiritual condition of this once godly nation. I know, however, that there is still hope for an awakening and healing of the land. One of the reasons I have this assurance is because God is still using watchmen to sound the alarm for prayer and action. Though reluctant to accept this title, Wale Babatunde is one of those watchmen. This book's warning is right, its sense of urgency is very appropriate, and if enough believers in England listen to and heed its call the dry bones of Britain can live again. Every Christian in the UK desperately needs to read *Awake Great Britain!*.

Dutch Sheets
Senior Pastor, Springs Harvest Fellowship
Colorado Springs, Colorado

Author's Preface

This book has been written with great grief in my heart. It is written with passion and love for the country of my adoption, Great Britain.

Over the last thirteen years I have seen this 'Christian' nation deliberately reject more and more of those Christian values as time goes by. I believe we will see crises develop as a consequence of our rejection of our spiritual heritage. *'Righteousness exalts a nation, but sin is a disgrace to any people'* (Proverbs 14:34, NIV).

More alarming still is that the Church in Britain seems oblivious of the situation and goes along with these decisions instead of making a stand. This book is therefore a wake up call for the slumbering Church in Britain to rise up out of apathy, indifference and deep spiritual slumber! It is a call to the remnant Church not to allow this nation to bleed to death!

We need a Jeremiah to weep over our sins; another John the Baptist to call us to repentance and another Elijah to bring fire down from heaven, so that multitudes across this nation may bow their knees to Jesus with the cry 'The Lord, He is God! The Lord, He is God!'

Wale Babatunde
October 2005

Introduction

In September 2004 I was invited to speak at a fellowship in Mendehall, Mississippi, USA. At the end of the week, after I had recovered from jet lag, I woke at three o'clock one morning. Sensing God wanted to speak to me, I spent some time in prayer. I began to feel a burden to call Julie Anderson, co-founder of Prayer for the Nations, in England. I picked up the phone, dialled London and across the Atlantic was Julie. After the usual greetings, she said, 'Wale, I have been thinking of you lately and I believe that God wants you to speak at a conference to be called "Awaken" in Westminster, London.

The message God gave me was not just for those who attended the conference, it is for a wider audience, it is for the whole nation. It is an important call to those of you who live in Great Britain, especially the Church. It is a wake up call at this time. The manuscript was in the final stages before printing when the events of 7/7 occurred. I believe the second wave of bombs that failed to work shows the protective power of prayer.

It's not for me to decide why I should be chosen to bring this unpalatable fare, just to be obedient when the master calls 'for such a time as this'. Here is my simple offering of loaves and fishes. I pray that the Lord will use this message to inspire and bless many people in this nation and beyond. Amen!

Wale Babatunde
October 2005

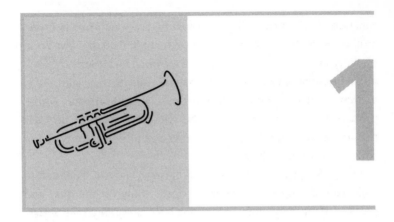

The Ministry of the Watchman

'... I have made you a watchman for the house of Israel; therefore you shall hear a word from My mouth and warn them for Me.'
(Ezekiel 33:7, NKJV)

In any army, modern or of the past, a vital defensive function is that of the watchman. While most of the troops are getting a necessary rest, someone has the important task of keeping watch so that the enemy does not sneak up and plant a bomb unbeknown to the company. The ancient Israelites had them on their journeys through the wilderness and continued to have them when they settled in the promised land and started to build homes for themselves.

We are engaged in a spiritual war with a sneaky enemy who would like to catch the Church unawares and destroy its reputation and authority. For this reason we need people who will act in the function of a lookout. Some have this as their prime function. A good example of a modern-day watchman is David Wilkerson of the Times Square Church in Manhattan, New York. I believe he has been called to be a watchman for America. A look at his ministry, messages and books will validate this claim. As in a modern army when there are times when someone whose primary function is something else will be required to do their turn on sentry duty. I believe this message I bring is from one of my turns on sentry duty.

Dutch Sheets, senior pastor at Springs Harvest Fellowship, Colorado Springs has done an excellent study on the duty and purpose of the watchman. In his book *Intercessory Prayer*, he writes:

> 'The term "watchman" ... was used to describe what we would today call "sentries", "guards" or "lookouts". These individuals were responsible for protecting primarily two things: vineyards or fields from thieves and animals, and cities from invading forces.
>
> Those watching crops were stationed on rocks, buildings or towers to provide a better range of vision. Towers or outposts in the fields usually had sleeping quarters because it was necessary to keep watch day and night during harvest. The watchmen would take shifts – one working, one sleeping – and thereby watch 24 hours a day ... These watchmen were also posted on the city walls, where they would function as sentries.' [1]

Let us look at the Bible passages Dutch Sheets uses as his selection of Old Testament references.

'For thus the Lord says to me,
"Go, station the lookout, let him report what he sees.
When he sees riders, horsemen in pairs,
A train of donkeys, a train of camels,
Let him pay close attention."

Then the lookout called,
"O Lord, I stand continually by day on the watchtower,
And I am stationed every night at my guard post." '
(Isaiah 21:6–8, NASB)

'Lift up a signal against the walls of Babylon;
Post a strong guard,
Station sentries,
Place men in ambush!
For the LORD *has both purpose and performed*
What he spoke concerning the inhabitants of Babylon.'
(Jeremiah 51:12, NASB)

'On your walls, O Jerusalem, I have appointed watchmen;
All day and all night they will never keep silent.
You who remind the LORD, *take no rest for yourselves.'*
(Isaiah 62:6, NASB)

Notice from the above passages that watchmen were people who were supposed to pay close attention to what was happening. Others may overlook things; others may ignore things, but not the watchmen. They were alert, trumpet in hand, ready. From the walls of the cities the watchmen were looking specifically for two things, messengers and enemies. When they saw a messenger in the distance they would give the appropriate signal to alert the gatekeeper to open the gate. 'Skilled watchmen could sometimes even recognise the runners by their stride before ever seeing their faces. In 2 Samuel 18:27 the watchman said, "the running . . . is like the running of Ahimaaz" '.[2]

The second duty of the watchman is to look out for the enemy on the way. When they saw danger ahead it was their responsibility to sound the alarm to warn the people, before the enemy could take them off guard. Sounding the trumpet well on time would rouse everyone to be ready to attack the enemy. We can see how important this function is in the Church. It is the responsibility of the watchmen to detect the scheming, the plans, and the plots of the enemy to attack the body, which could be fatal! They are to warn the troops – the body, the Church, so that we are not taken unawares.

Ezekiel, a watchman

'The word of the LORD came to me, "Son of man, speak to your countrymen and say to them: 'When I bring the sword against the land, and the people of the land choose one of their men and make him their watchman, and he sees the sword coming against the land and blows the trumpet to warn the people, then if anyone hears the trumpet but does not take warning and the sword comes and takes his life, his blood will be on his own head. Since he heard the sound of the trumpet but did not take warning, his blood will be on his own head. If he had taken warning, he would have saved himself. But if the watchman sees the sword coming and does not blow the trumpet to warn the people and the sword comes and takes the life of one of them, that man will be taken away because of his sin, but I will hold the watchman accountable for his blood.' " '

(Ezekiel 33:1–6, NIV)

Again in Ezekiel 3:16–19, we read:

'At the end of seven days the word of the LORD came to me, "Son of man, I have made you a watchman for the house of Israel; so hear the word I speak and give them warning from me. When I say to the wicked man, 'You will surely die,' and you do not warn him or speak out to dissuade him from his evil ways in order to save his life, that wicked man will die for his sin, and I will hold you accountable for his blood. But if you do warn the wicked man and

*he does not turn from his wickedness or from his evil ways, he will
die for his sin; but you will have saved yourself." '*

(NIV)

From the above scriptures we can see that the watchman had a
very serious assignment from God. It was an assignment he could
not take lightly because it had divine consequences. First, he was
to speak what he had seen or been shown. The watchman had a
mandate under God to speak and warn them of coming dangers.
His assignment was to blow the trumpet, to wake up, to alert
the people of the dangers ahead. The purpose of warnings was
to make people ready to defeat the enemy. His warnings were to
ward off enemies. It was meant to alert the people to inherent
danger.

After he had blown the trumpet and delivered the message, if
the people took no notice, then he was clear before God. He's not
guilty of the consequences that follow! After God has sent a
message, and it has been rightly delivered, what we do with it
becomes our personal and corporate responsibility. The consequence for refusal to blow the trumpet in the face of danger was
so serious as to warrant divine sanction! God holds you accountable for his blood. How many times has God given so many of us
a word to deliver to a fellowship, leader or a political leader and
yet we took it lightly? Remember, it is a fearful thing to fall into
the hands of the living God.

You might ask, 'What bearing does the function of the
watchman have with the message in this book?' I can give you a
simple answer, but first let me say categorically that I don't
believe I stand in the office of a watchman, neither do I have any
pretentious desire to be called one. However, the message that
God has given to me in this book is that of a watchman. It is not
primarily a message of instruction or doctrine, I do not really
consider it a prophetic message nor do I see it as a message to
encourage the Body of Christ. I see the message of this book as a

wake-up call, a call to alert the Church, a message to warn you of the enemies within, a message to warn about what you might have overlooked; a message that I believe we might pay dearly for if we ignore it. It is a message to church leaders across denominations and theological convictions.

This book is a message to all members of the Body of Christ, full-time workers, Christian businessmen, full-time home makers, nursing mothers, praying women, intercessors, young and old, including children! My prayer is that we all will respond appropriately.

Suggested practical action

▶ Pray that God will wake up His watchmen for this country to hear from God and warn us to be ready.

▶ Pray for the spirit of boldness to come upon our watchmen so they can declare boldly what God is showing them without fear of man (see 1 Timothy 1:7; Acts 4:13–20).

▶ For further reading I recommend *Intercessory Prayer* by Dutch Sheets (see note 1 on p. 183 for details).

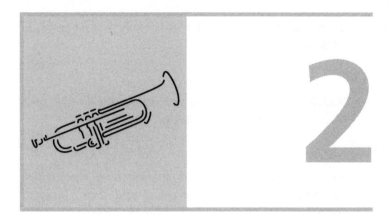

What is the Time?

'And that, knowing the time, that now it is high time to awake out of sleep: for now is our salvation nearer than when we believed.'
(Romans 13:11, KJV)

Time is indispensable to life. You cannot function in life without being aware of time passing. Our lives, unlike that of God who is infinite, are ruled by events happening in time. There is an appropriate time for everything. I believe we are in danger of getting our activity clock out of sync with God's intentions for us at the present time.

The verse that starts this chapter is a vital key to our understanding of the times we live in. I would like to review several versions to obtain every nuance of meaning of this important subject. We need to be conscious of the spiritual atmosphere we live in today.

'Do this, knowing the time, that it is already the hour for you to awaken from sleep . . . '

(NASB)

'And do this, understanding the present time. The hour has come for you to wake up from your slumber . . . '

(NIV)

'Besides this you know what [a critical] hour this is, how it is high time now for you to wake up out of your sleep – rouse to reality . . . '

(Amplified)

We all understand the importance of time; our daily, weekly, monthly and yearly activities are dictated by time. Time is indispensable to life. A life spent ignoring time will be characterized by chaos and confusion. Most people, children and adults, have a daily routine based on time. For example, when my children wake up in the morning they get washed and dressed and ready for school. Then they have breakfast. After breakfast we have a time of family devotion and they are then taken to school. They are expected to be ready at 9:00am. If they arrive late, they will be told off. They stay in school from just before 9:00am and finish at 5:00pm. After school they are either taken home to eat, to rest, do their allotted cleaning at home and then start their homework, or if it is the night of our mid-week service they are brought to my office to attend fellowship together. You can see that young as my children are, they operate in a routine dictated by time.

The same applies to most adults of working age. We wake up around the same time each day and after the usual preparations head for our work. Most of us spend an average of eight hours or more every day at work. Unless something unusual happens, this is the routine of most adults. Most of us are back home around 7:00pm, spend the evening with our family eating, watching TV, going to fellowship or attending the gym for work-out sessions.

On another level there are certain things, activities, assignments that we do in seasons. These are longer periods of time during which our function is to do certain specific things. From the age of five we start primary school and attend school until sixteen. During our late teens we attend universities or higher institutions of education to qualify for a profession or trade, or attempt to find a job. By the age of thirty most adults, at least in the Western world, will have passed through some form of higher education. You would not see a thirty-year-old man enrolling at a primary school. He's starting education at the wrong time. The same would apply if you saw a woman of seventy attending the antenatal clinic, expecting a baby. This would be highly irregular! It could only be a miracle because it is the wrong time of her life. Doctors say the optimum time for women to conceive and give birth to children is from twenty to thirty-five years of age. Naturally we would expect most babies when the mother is between her mid teens and forty-five years of age. When you get to the extremes of the age range you find more complications arising. All this goes to show that time is crucial to our existence and activities. It can be just as necessary to realize our ministry functions will alter over time.

Has anyone ever stopped you on the road or in the bus, tube or in the shopping mall with the question 'What is the time, please'? I guarantee you, they had an activity they meant to carry out and were simply checking to make sure that they were on schedule. They are aware that ten minutes late may mean missing their flight or an important appointment that may cost them several thousand pounds.

If I were to ask those of you reading this book now the question, 'What is the time?', with a glance at your watch your answer will be immediate. 'It's 9:00am or 12:35pm,' or 'Ten to nine.' You only have to take a look at the clock to say what the exact time is. However, if I were to ask you, 'What is the time spiritually?', I wonder how many of you could give me an answer.

Dr Morris Cerullo says 'All truth is parallel', meaning, as it is in the natural world so it is in the spiritual. I wonder again how many Christian leaders, apostles, prophets, evangelists, pastors and teachers know what time it is spiritually. As I have said earlier, time dictates our activities. If we don't know the time, how can we function effectively? If we don't understand spiritual timing, how can we fit into God's divine programme or agenda? Are we going to be carrying out assignments for this season rather than remaining firmly in the assignment of yesteryear? If we are ignorant of divine timing, how do we know that the cloud of glory has moved on and we are to move on with the next phase of God's programme? Like Samuel, when God says, 'I am through with Saul, it's a new season, the season of David. It's time to stop crying and mourning over Saul,' how are we to know it's time to stop crying for Saul if we don't understand divine timing?

The writer of Ecclesiastes says,

> 'There is a time for everything,
>   and a season for every activity under heaven.'
>
> (Ecclesiastes 3:1, NIV)

Again I would stress this by looking at some of the other Bible versions:

> 'There is an appointed time for everything. And there is a time for every event under heaven.'
>
> (NASB)

> 'To every thing there is a season, and a time to every purpose under the heaven.'
>
> (KJV)

'To every thing there is a season, and a time for every matter or
purpose under heaven.'

(Amplified)

He goes further to highlight the circle of activities that occurs
in our lives at various times and season. Verses 2–7 read:

'a time to be born and a time to die,
a time to plant and a time to uproot,
a time to kill and a time to heal,
a time to tear down and a time to build,
a time to weep and a time to laugh,
a time to mourn and a time to dance,
a time to scatter stones and a time to gather them,
a time to embrace and a time to refrain,
a time to search and a time to give up,
a time to keep and a time to throw away,
a time to tear and a time to mend,
a time to be silent and a time to speak.'

(NIV)

There's a time for everything

In life there's a time to sleep or rest and there's a time for work or
a time to be active. Even God worked for a season and afterwards
rested. Our bodies have an inbuilt daily rhythm. At dawn we
begin to wake up, at dusk we start to feel sleepy. After a hard, long
day of work the natural thing is for us to sleep. If we sleep during
the day, when we are expected to be at work, others might think
we were sick or at least notice that something was wrong. Then
again they might conclude we were just being lazy.

The same thing applies spiritually. We should not be asleep
when we have the Great Commission to fulfil! We cannot afford
to fall into a state of spiritual stupor when we are supposed to be

watching and waiting for the Bridegroom's coming. This was what Paul meant when he wrote to the Christians in Rome when he charged them to wake up, *'Besides this you know what [a critical] hour this is, how it is high time now for you to wake up out of your sleep – rouse to reality . . . '* (Romans 13:11, Amplified).

When Paul was writing this, he had in mind the return of Jesus Christ, either at the end of the world, or at death. For the individual the two amount to the same. Whether Christ comes while we are alive and we are caught up to meet Him in the air, or whether it be at death that we are taken immediately into the presence of Jesus our Saviour, we are to be ready to meet Christ when the call comes. According to Paul the alarm has already sounded to waken believers who have slept in the world, in carnality and compromise. In a day that the devil is on rampage we cannot afford to sleep. In order to know what the time is we need to go to the Bible and discover what the time is.

> *'For it is light that makes everything visible. This is why it is said:*
>
> *"Wake up o sleeper,*
> *rise from the dead,*
> *and Christ will shine in you."*
>
> *Be very careful, then, how you live – not as unwise but as wise, making the most of every opportunity, because the days are evil.'*
> (Ephesians 5:14–16, NIV)

It does not matter how optimistic we are or what our eschatological persuasions are, there are enough scriptures to point out to us that we are living in evil days. Just look around today and see the way in which evil is escalating. Take a look for yourself and see the way evil is increasing. Things that used to be reckoned as evil or sin some decades ago are not only perceived today as good, but are backed up by legislation. How much evil is on the increase!

'But mark this: There will be terrible times in the last days.'
                                    (2 Timothy 3:1, NIV)

I believe when Paul wrote this epistle almost two thousand years ago, he thought the last days had already begun, that living during those days was proof enough. However, I believe that the last days that he's referring to here are the very last days just before the second coming of Jesus Christ. In other words he was referring to our days. Paul said there would be terrible times, those days would be difficult, times of trouble. It will be a time of great stress. It will be a time that things will be hard to deal with and to bear. It will be a time in which men's hearts will fail them for what is coming upon the earth. They will be days when it will be difficult, if not nigh impossible, to live righteously in the world.

I believe we are living in a time of the devil's great wrath. The devil, our arch-enemy and the accuser of the brethren, has always been evil, wicked and ferocious, but I believe we are living in a day that the devil is even more ferocious because he knows his time is short; because Jesus is about to come back. Because the devil will soon be punished for all his age-long atrocities, he's trying to do as much damage as possible. He wants to make sure he attacks as many believers as possible, he wants to make sure the gospel does not get to unsaved folks, he wants to make sure that false cults, religions are released on earth in order to deceive as many people as possible. The devil is definitely on the rampage today.

'And I heard a loud voice saying in heaven, Now is come salvation, and strength, and the kingdom of our God, and the power of his Christ: for the accuser of our brethren is cast down, which accused them before our God day and night. And they overcame him by the blood of the lamb, and by the word of their testimony; and they loved not their lives unto death. Therefore rejoice, ye heavens, and

ye that dwell in them. Woe to the inhabiters of the earth and of the sea! for the devil is come down unto you, having great wrath, because he knoweth that he hath but a short time.'

(Revelation 12:10–12, KJV)

I believe when Isaiah wrote in the sixtieth chapter that darkness will cover the earth and thick darkness the people, he was writing about our time.

'*See, darkness covers the earth
    and thick darkness is over the peoples . . . '*

(Isaiah 60:2, NIV)

This is the time in which we are living today – evil days, perilous times, times of thick darkness, and the time of the devil's great wrath. However, these are the days of God's power. These are the days of the manifestation of the sons of God! These are also the days of unprecedented harvest. These are the days of transformation in the nations.

In order to know spiritual timing we need discernment. O that God will grace us with the gift of discernment! O that God will deliver us from spiritual dullness! Jesus, during His earthly ministry, rebuked the religious folk of His day for being able to forecast the weather, but lacking in spiritual discernment. Are there not many religious leaders today who are leading God's heritage, but lack spiritual discernment? Listen to Jesus' rebuke:

'*And he said also to the people, When ye see a cloud rise out of the west, straightaway ye say, There cometh a shower; and so it is. And when ye see the south wind blow, ye say, There will be heat; and it cometh to pass. Ye hypocrites, ye can discern the face of the sky and of the earth; but how is it that ye do not discern this time?*

(Luke 12:54–56, KJV)

I like Charles B. Williams' version of the New Testament that puts it this way: *'how is it that you can not discern the present crisis?'* [3] The Knox version says *'the times you live in'*, while the NEB says *'this fateful hour'*.

Needed in this time of crisis, in this fateful hour are men and women of discernment, saints who know the exact time in the divine clock.

The tribe of Issachar

Recently the Spirit of the Lord has been pointing out the relevance of one of the tribes of Israel to the Church today. This tribe had a unique function, a very useful one for political decisions for Israel.

> *'And of the children of Issachar, which were men that had understanding of the times, to know what Israel ought to do.'*
>
> (1 Chronicles 12:32a, KJV)

From the tribe of Issachar were 200 leaders of the tribe, all men who understood the temper of the times and knew the best course for Israel to take.

> *'Of Israel, 200 of their leaders who had understanding of the times and knew what Israel should do.'*
>
> (Berkeley)

Notice with me something very significant about the children of Issachar. They were men or leaders who had understanding of the times. This is very important. This characteristic is very crucial at this hour. This quality is indispensable at this fateful hour. Needed at this hour are clear prophetic voices. We need to find those people who have this function in the people of God today. The Church is tired of speculation; we are tired of guesswork. What is the time now in Great Britain? What is the time now in Europe? What season are we in today? What time is it economically? What time is it politically? What time is it for the Church? Are there not prophets in the land? God, please speak so that we can have Your direction.

I think there is much confusion in the Body, because we are not sure of the time. It seems we are engaged in some programmes that do not have divine sanction. Some people are pursuing certain relationships, unaware that in God's timing those relationships will not help to fulfil our assignment for this hour. Spiritual timing always informs spiritual activities. How can we do the Spirit's bidding for this hour when we don't understand spiritual timing?

The children of Issachar knew exactly what Israel ought to be doing because they had understanding of the times. Understanding of the times will affect a number of things; our programmes, prayers, partnerships, personal matters and strategies. Our disposition and the way we act in a time of peace will be quite different during a time of war. These are the days of war. Why are we acting as though it is peace time? This is the time that the name of our Lord and Saviour is being blasphemed and yet the Church is silent. What is the strategy for taking Great Britain back to God? What response should we make as leaders to ungodly edicts issuing from Europe?

The Church, God's people, are looking to their leaders for strategy and vision, for worthy leadership at this hour – yet it doesn't seem many understand the times, let alone what we should be doing. May the Lord open our eyes and grant us discerning hearts to know what time it is, so that we may be able to do the Spirit's bidding.

Suggested practical action

▶ Read the following scriptures in as many versions as possible, taking time to meditate on them: Romans 13:11; Ecclesiastes 3:1–8; Ephesians 5:14–16; Luke 13:54–56; 1 Chronicles 12:32a.

▶ Pray for the spirit of discernment to become operational in your life and the lives of Christian leaders.

▶ Pray for the Issachar anointing to begin to operate more and more in the lives of believers and Christian leaders in the UK.

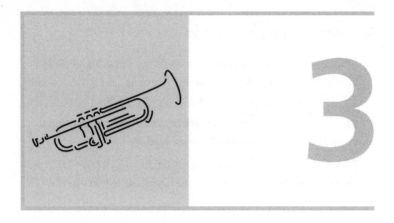

A Time of Crisis

'For from the least of them even unto the greatest of them every one is given to covetousness; and from the prophet even unto the priest every one dealeth falsely.

They have healed also the hurt of the daughter of my people slightly, saying, Peace, Peace; when there is no peace.

*Were they ashamed when they had committed abomination? nay, they were not at all ashamed, neither could they blush: therefore they shall fall among them that fall: at the time that I visit them they shall be cast down, saith the L*ORD*.*

*Thus saith the L*ORD*, Stand ye in the ways, and see, and ask for the old paths, where is the good way, and walk therein, and ye shall find rest for your souls. But they said, We will not walk therein.'*
(Jeremiah 6:13–16, KJV)

There are many good things happening in Great Britain at the moment. All around us are signs of hope. We are experiencing growth in some segments of the Church. We see some ministries entering debate with society in key areas such as politics, justice and education, but let no-one be deceived, the Christian Church in Great Britain is in crisis. We find ourselves at a crossroads. I believe there are few times in the history of the Church in this nation that can be compared to these times.

Is this relevant to me personally? Is there really anything new happening in Britain today compared to previous times? Is there anything I can do to influence the whole nation? Well, I answer you like this, 'As it is in the Church, so it is in the nation.' In every generation the nation always reflects the Church. Your beliefs and behaviour are followed by attitudes and behaviour in society. In every nation the decisions the Church makes influence the nation, for good or ill.

Some people cannot see anything wrong in the Church. To say that the Church in Britain is going through a period of crisis is just being alarmist. I have even heard such attitudes coming from people heading up large denominations. What I find most alarming is that even the ones from whom you would expect a shaft of light to shine seem to be fast asleep. 'Give us some evidence to show that Great Britain is in a state of crisis,' some of you may ask.

On Friday 27 October 2000, the former Archbishop of Canterbury and former head of the Anglican Communion of England and worldwide declared on the front page of the *Daily Telegraph* 'Britain now a society of atheists'.

In his equally pessimistic view about the state of Christianity in Britain, Cardinal Murphy O'Connor, leader of the Roman Catholic Church in England and Wales, remarked in September 2001 that Christianity is close to being vanquished in Britain and no longer influences the government or people's lives. He further stated that Christianity as a background to people's lives and moral decisions and to the government and the social life of Britain has almost been vanquished.[4] Furthermore, even as recently as January 2003, the Cardinal in an interview remarked, 'Britain has become a pagan country over the past half century, creating a vacuum in which people will believe in anything.'[5]

Recently I was in the Houses of Parliament at a meeting organized by the Maranatha Community to launch their prayer initiative on the state of the nation. They presented a great deal of interesting factual evidence on the spiritual state of this nation. I want to reproduce some of their statements, with their kind permission, for two reasons: first, to contradict those who think it's just me just crying wolf. Second, I want you to join me in prayer. The picture I paint is not just my own. There are other people also who can see the true spiritual picture of our nation. Many people, I believe, are unaware of the true situation that we are faced with today. I am giving useful information to those who love this nation and are praying for a return to biblical standards. For those who are earnestly working and praying for transformation this will give you something to get your teeth into. This information is to be used to inform your intercession, to empower your petitions in the heavenlies. It is meant to give prayer pointers for all the praying saints across this island. Here are the facts – I hope they will send you to your knees!

EVIDENCE

The State of our Nation Today

Suffering Children

- Over 60,000 children live in care; 98% are admitted due to family breakdown. (*Department of Health, 2002 ref 2002/0193*)
- 32,465 children and young people were on the child protection register for the year ending March 2003. (*Statistics of Education: Referrals, Assessments and Children and Young People, 2004, DfES*)
- There are 384,200 children in England alone categorised as 'in need'. (*Ibid.*)
- Over 110,000 adults have convictions for sex offences against children. (*NSPCC Child Protection HelpLine publication 2003*)
- In the summer term, 2003, there were 82,400 expulsions from schools in England & Wales, 14% due to violence against another pupil. (*Permanent*

and Fixed Period Exclusions, Summer Term 2002/3, Experimental Statistics First Release, DFES, 29.7.04)

- 100,000 children run away from home every year. (*Children's Society, 2001*)
- 1 in 3 (4.4 million) children are living in poverty, compared with 1 in 10 in 1979. (*Child Poverty Action Group Briefing, February 2000*)
- 17% of 15 year olds and 6% of 13–14 year olds in England attended NHS Family Planning clinics in 2003/4. (*NHS Contraceptive Services, Statistical Bulletin, 29th September 2004*)
- Nearly 1.3 million children now have parents with addiction problems. (*Institute for Alcohol Studies, 2004; ACMD, 2003*)
- There were 846 abductions and attempted abductions of children in Britain in 2002–03 – up from 584 in 2001–02. (*Home Office R&D Statistics Division 1.3.04*)
- More than 30,000 children rang ChildLine in 2003 about bullying – 10,000 more than the previous year. (*ChildLine 25.8.04*)
- 18% of children under 15 are now obese. (*Health Development Agency 8.10.03*)
- Teenage asthma rates in Britain are the highest in the world. 33.6% of 13–14 year olds now suffer from it. There are now 10 million sufferers in Britain and Ireland. (*Global Institute for Arthritis Research February 2004*)

Marriage Breakdown

- The number of divorces has nearly doubled since 1971, from 80,000 to 157,000. (*Social Trends 34, 2004, Office of National Statistics*)
- The United Kingdom has the third highest divorce rate in Europe. (*Eurostat, Social Trends 34, 2004, Office of National Statistics*)
- 25% of divorces in 2001 occurred within 5 years. (*Series FM2 No. 29, Marriage, Divorce & Adoption Statistics, ONS, 2003*)
- 30% of divorces in 2001 involved people divorced in a previous marriage. (*Series FM2 No. 29, Marriage, Divorce & Adoption Statistics, ONS, 2003*)
- The direct and indirect cost of family breakdown to the economy is approaching £30 billion a year. (*The Cost of Family Breakdown, 2000, Family Matters Institute*)

Dysfunctional Families

- Births outside marriage have increased from 12% to 41% between 1980 and 2002. (*Social Trends 34, ONS*)
- The number of single parent families increased from 8% in 1971 to 23% in 2003. (*Social Trends 34, ONS*)
- Up to 40% of fathers lose contact with their children within two years of separation. (*Children First Consultation Paper, DSS, 1998*)

- 90% of births to teenage mothers are outside marriage. (*ONS 2001; Kirby, 2002*)
- 1.75 million children are being raised in single parent families. (*Population Trends 109, ONS 2002*)
- Three-quarters of a million British children have no contact with their fathers following the breakdown of their relationship. (*FPSC Survey of Lone Parents*)
- 1 in 4 children affected by divorce are under 5, two thirds are under 10. (*Social Trends 34, 2004, ONS*)
- The UK has the highest rate of teenage pregnancy in Europe, 40% higher than Portugal in 2nd place. (*Social Trends 33, 2003, ONS*)
- Young offenders now constitute one third of all criminal convictions. (*ONS, 2004*)
- More than half of convicted young offenders have absent fathers (*Wasted Lives Report co-authored by the Chief Executive of NACRO 1998*)

Life Destroyed
- 23% of conceptions ended in legal abortions in 2000. (*Social Trends 33, 2003, ONS*)
- There were 6,024,221 abortions in England, Wales & Scotland between 1968 & 2003. (*Government Statistical Service August 2004 & ISD Scotland*)
- There were 181,600 abortions in 2003, 80% were NHS funded. (*Government Statistical Service August 2004*)
- 75% of abortions are carried out on single women. (*Statistical Bulletin, Abortion Statistics in England & Wales, DoH 2002*)

Cries for Help
- Each year 140,000 people attempt to commit suicide. (*Community Care, 9.10.03*)
- Every day 4,000 children call ChildLine. Since it was formed in 1986, it has counselled over 1 million children. (*ChildLine 2004*).
- Last year the Samaritans answered 4.6 million calls from people in despair – one every seven seconds. (*Samaritans 2004*)

Crime that pays
- Only 1 in 16 criminals face conviction. (*Route to Justice, Audit Commission, 2002*)
- It is estimated that fewer than 1 in 50 sexual offences against children result in conviction. (*Joseph Rowntree Foundation Report, 15.11.04*)

Lawlessness and Disorder
- The prison population in England and Wales is at an all-time high of 73,688 (30th January 2004) an increase of 25,000 in the last 10 years and an increase of 2,729 in the past year. Home Office projections

predicate a prison population of between 91,400 and 91,600 by the end of the decade. (*Home Office Statistics 2004*)

- Less than 100,000 offences were recorded in England and Wales annually before the 1920s. By 1950 the level was half a million. By 1980 this had risen to 2.5 million and in 2002/3 the BCS recorded 12.3 million crimes. (*Crime in England & Wales 2002–2003, H.O.2004*)
- Annual criminal acts are now approximately 60 million: confirmed by Jon Simmons, Head of the Home Office's Crime Statistics Unit. (*Civitas; Nov. 2002*)
- 36% of males aged 18–21 admit to committing an offence in the last year. (*Home Office Research Study 209*)
- 27% of people were victims of crime in 2002–2003. (*Crime In England & Wales 2002–3, H.O., 2004*)
- There are approximately 31 million acts of shoplifting every year. (*The Economic and Social Costs of Crime, Home Office, 2000*)
- The total cost of retail crime is estimated to be £2,200 million a year. (*British Retail Consortium, 10th Retail Crime Survey, 2001/2*)
- More than 50,000 pupils play truant every day. (*DfES, September 2003*)

Violence
- There was a group sex attack for every day in London in 2003. (*Scotland Yard Report January 2004*)
- Offences involving firearms have doubled since 1997. (*Social Trends 34, ONS*)
- Between 1987 and 2000 there has been a 500% increase in operations where firearms have been issued to police (2,185 to 10,913). (*Lords Hansard, 17.3.98 Statistics on the Police use of firearms in England & Wales 1999/2000, H.O.*)
- One in ten doctors are physically assaulted by patients or their relatives every year. One in three doctors experienced some kind of physical or verbal violence in the past year. (*BMA report, 'Violence at work: the experience of UK doctors', Health Policy and Economic Research Unit, October 2003*)
- Crime reported on trains, stations and railway property rose from 107,769 in 1998–1999 to 123,463 in 2003–2004. The detection fell from 30% to 21%. During this period sex attacks leapt from 719 to 1120. (*British Transport Police, May 2004*)
- 10 children a day were expelled in 2003 for assaults. (*DfES 13.7.04*)
- There were 116,000 violent or abusive incidents against NHS staff recorded in 2002/03 – a 38% rise in two years. (*Department of Health 14.3.04*)
- 1 in 5 children have experienced bullying at school in the last 12 months. (*NCPTA, November 2004*)

The Scourge of Drugs

- Cocaine use has doubled in Britain in the past seven years. (*Independent Drug Monitoring Unit 19.7.04*)
- 11–15 year olds taking drugs in England have doubled in number since 1998. (*Smoking, Drinking and Drug Use amongst Young People 2003, National Centre for Social Research/National Foundation for Education Research*)
- People reporting to Drug Misuse Agencies in England have doubled in number since 1993. (*Regional Drug Misuse Database 6 months ending March 2001*)
- 26,000 drug offences were recorded in 1987. In 1998 there were 128,000 offences recorded. (*Drugscope Online*)
- There was a 27% increase in drug trafficking and possession offences in London for 2002/03. (*Metropolitan Police Crime Statistic 13.7.03*)
- More than five million people regularly use cannabis, 3.4m take Ecstasy and 2m amphetamines and cocaine. Two in five people between 25 & 34, and more than a third of those between 35 & 44 say they have taken unlawful drugs. (*Observer/ICM poll 21.4.02*)
- Research suggests that 60% of drug-addicted mothers and 85% of fathers no longer look after their children. (*Drug Misuse Research Project, Glasgow University 2004*)

A danger signal – family breakdown

I want to draw your attention to something that I believe is the greatest problem confronting British society. I'm confident most people agree with me that the institution of the family is the bedrock of any society. The family institution as we have known it for many centuries is on the verge of collapse in the United Kingdom. Many problems that we have in this nation today stem from this one fundamental issue – family breakdown.

There is plenty of evidence to show that the type of upbringing you had as a child affects your health, education, even the likelihood you might use alcohol or drugs or even whether you are more or less likely to end up in prison. Statistics have shown that a large percentage of children who end up in care homes or prisons use drugs, or are involved in violence are from dysfunctional families.

In spite of the overwhelming evidence that the institution of the family – by that I mean those living in the traditional unit of father (male) and mother (female), with children of their joint genetic union – is the best place to raise children, our government is noticeably anti-marriage in its policies. There are many people in the cabinet and government who are totally opposed to the idea of marriage as laid down in the Word of God, and as we have known it for centuries.

The present state of the Church

'I know your deeds, that you are neither cold nor hot. I wish you were either one or the other!'

(Revelation 3:15, NIV)

'Here I am! I stand at the door and knock. If anyone hears my voice and opens the door, I will come in and eat with him, and he with me.'

(Revelation 3:20, NIV)

'Yet I hold this against you: You have forsaken your first love. Remember the height from which you have fallen! Repent and do the things you did at first. If you do not repent, I will come to you and remove your lampstand from its place.'

(Revelation 2:4–5, NIV)

These were the warnings from the risen Lord to the Laodicean Church and to the Church in Ephesus. What alarms me is that this is the same situation I see in the Church in Britain today; we are lax, loose, lazy and lukewarm. If we have a large bank balance, or a successful ministry or a magnificent building to conduct worship in, we assume we have God's approval and endorsement of our behaviour. Well, hear what the Lord said to the Laodicean church:

> *'But you do not realize that you are wretched, pitiful, poor, blind and naked.'*
>
> (Revelation 3:17b, NIV)

The Church today, in the words of veteran preacher and mentor George Verwer, founder of Operation Mobilization, is 'God's holy frozen people'.

There is decay in the Church today; with only a few exceptions we are in decline. There is terrible apathy and powerlessness in our churches. The spirit of unbelief pervades the atmosphere, and many of God's people are battle-weary, tired and frustrated. Today we are indifferent to the plight of many thousands of people going to a Christ-less eternity. Where are the soldiers of the cross, the army of soul winners, snatching people out of hell fire? Where are the people taking the Great Commission seriously?

Leonard Ravenhill wrote:

> 'Could a mariner sit idle if he heard the drowning cry?
> Could a doctor sit in comfort and just let his patients
>   die?
> Could a fireman sit idle, let men burn and give no hand?
> Can you sit at ease in Zion with the world around
>   you DAMNED?' [6]

The wake-up call

We believe God is calling His people in this land to wake up, to hear His words and to face up to the extreme seriousness of the spiritual condition of our nation and our churches today.

With kind permission from the Maranatha Community, I reproduce a wake-up call from the Lord to the Church at large in the UK. May the Lord use it to rouse us up form our slumber.

We are asleep and in danger of dying in our sleep.
God is calling us to wake up!
Our hearts are cold.
God wants to bring the warmth of His love into our being.
We are half lovers.
God wants us to be consumed with passion for His kingdom.
We are half givers.
God gave all for us and wants us to withhold nothing from Him.
We are half believers.
God wants to hear our 'Yes'.
We are blind to the reality of dying churches and dying culture.
God wants to open our eyes.
We are deaf to His words and to the cry of the needy.
God wants to unstop our ears.
We are dumb in the face of injustice, idolatry and denial of life.
God wants to anoint our lips and end our deafening silence.
We are soiled with the ways of the world.
God wants to pour His cleansing waters over us.
We are in darkness.
God wants His light to shine on us, within us and through us.
We look inward, consumed with self.
God calls us to look out, meeting Him in others.

We look down in depression and despair.
**God calls us to look up and be overwhelmed with
      His glory.**
We look back, obsessed with the past.
**God calls us to look forward with hope and
      expectation.**
We are embracing a culture of death, decay and
      hopelessness.
God calls us to newness and life.
We are separated from each other in our selfish
      individualism.
God calls us to come together as one.
We are old and tired.
God comes to make all things new.
We are surrounded by lies and deceit.
God wants us to embrace His truth.
Our roots are dry and there is little life within us.
**God wants us to water our roots to bring blossom
      and fruit.**
We consume poison, damaging us in body, mind and
      spirit.
God invites us to receive the Bread of Life.[7]

Suggested practical action

▶ Spend fifteen minutes a day thanking God for the things He is
  birthing in our nation such as the 24/7 prayer network. You
  can contact them via www.24-7prayer.com

▶ Pray through the information in this chapter on the state
  of this nation. Please bring this information to the attention of
  your pastor or elders and ask them to use them as prayer
  points in your services. For further information see:
      www.maranathacommunity.org.uk

▶ Read a newspaper or listen to the news daily and write or talk to your Member of Parliament when legislation is proposed that is against Christian values, especially when it might have a detrimental effect on the family, asking for their views and what they propose to do.

▶ Pray for the Church to be awake to the times we are living in (see Revelation 3:15).

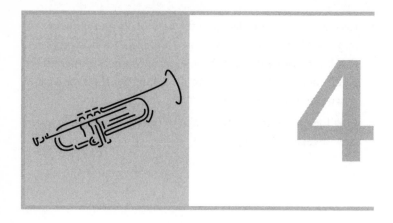

A Call to Prayer

'Up, said he, and cry out upon God!'
(Jonah 1:6a, Knox)

The book of Jonah is small compared to most books of the Old Testament. Its message though is highly significant for us today because it reveals fundamental things about God. We can never successfully run away from God. God often does His greatest works through the most unlikely candidates. Another lesson we learn from the book is that regardless of patriotism, we must never put our nations before God. Regardless of our nationality, race or origin, God loves us.

> *'The word of the LORD came to Jonah son of Amittai: "Go to the great city of Nineveh, go now and denounce it, for its wickedness stares me in the face." But Jonah set out for Tarshish to escape from the LORD. He went down to Joppa, where he found a ship*

bound for Tarshish. He paid his fare and went on board, meaning to travel by it to Tarshish out of reach of the LORD. *But the* LORD *let loose a hurricane, and the sea ran so high in the storm that the ship threatened to break up. The sailors were afraid, and each called to his god for help. Then they threw things overboard to lighten the ship. Jonah had gone down into a corner of the ship and was lying sound asleep when the captain came upon him. "What, sound asleep?" he said "Get up, and call on your god; perhaps he will spare us a thought and we shall not perish." '*

(Jonah 1:1–6, NEB)

Did Jonah do as he was told? No, Jonah ran away from the Lord and headed for Tarshish. He went down to Joppa and got on a ship going in the opposite direction. He thought he could get away from God, but God sees us wherever we are. The Lord had plans for Jonah that He intended him to carry out.

The sailors were afraid and each cried out to his own God. They threw the cargo into the sea to lighten the ship. Meanwhile where was Jonah? Fast asleep in his cabin. Eventually the captain went and woke Jonah up saying, *'Get up and call on your god! Maybe he will take notice of us, and we will not perish'* (Jonah 1:6, NIV)

Jonah was called by God on a clear prophetic and missionary assignment: *'Go to the great city of Nineveh and preach against it . . . '* (Jonah 1:1, NIV).

Jonah's mission, assignment, and job description was very clear, even the place of his assignment was specified – Nineveh. Jonah was supposed to be busy carrying out his Master's bidding, however he was disobedient. He did not go to Nineveh; he went in the opposite direction. I wonder what he was going to do in Tarshish.

This seems to be the position the Church is in today. We have a clear assignment from the Lord, but how many of us are faithfully carrying out our duties?

Many servants of God, called and commissioned, anointed and appointed from heaven, have been side-tracked from their God-given assignment. Some have been caught up in pleasure and leisure, and the attractions that the world offers, others have been too busy doing business or any activity but that ordained by heaven. Jonah likewise was heading for the wrong location. I cannot just overlook that, the Holy Spirit inside me does not permit me to. Too many of God's servants today are in the wrong place. There is a place of planting for every minister and ministry. God is the one who calls, equips and sends.

Do you know the saying, 'Some are sent others simply went'? Servant of God, as you read this book, ask yourself are you rightly located? Have you uprooted yourself from where God planted you? Some of you may have relocated because you heard that there's greener pasture in a particular nation or city! Some of you may have been told that you can build a mega ministry if you relocate to Europe, America, Canada or Great Britain.

May God deliver us from spiritual short-sightedness and carnality.

Notice with me the situation at sea. There was such a violent storm that not only was the ship going to break up, but the lives of all those on board were in danger. This is exactly the situation in Europe. There is great storm brewing over all institutions, education, health care, politics, media and even the very foundation of society, the family. Such is the storm that the lives of countless millions of people are in danger. Lives have been, and will continue to be, destroyed through the state murder law called abortion. Our children are being corrupted by watching pornographic and violent films. Lives are in danger because the NHS is overstretched and morale sapped by adverse publicity and erosion of income. Lives will be destroyed by legalizing cannabis. Eternal lives are in danger because of rejection of Christ. The government is doing all it can to destroy our Judeo-Christian heritage that was handed down to us.

It was bad enough that there was a storm at sea, with the lives of those on board in danger of perishing, yet what I found more shocking was that Jonah, God's servant, was fast asleep. How could Jonah be asleep in the midst of a storm so bad that lives were in imminent danger? How was it possible for everyone to be awake except Jonah? Jonah, where did you get the confidence from to be snoring in the midst of danger when you were living in disobedience to God?

Jonah represents the Church. Society today is in a state of crisis with everyone running around perplexed, shouting, crying, and screaming for help, yet the Church is fast asleep. What I find so disturbing is that all the other people in the ship were awake, only Jonah was fast asleep. This typifies what is happening today. Many people who don't know Jesus as Lord are more alive than believers. Unbelievers will petition and fight for the rights of unborn children, not the Church. Unbelievers protest against pornography, not the Church. Pastors are too spiritual to be concerned about mundane things. We are too heavenly minded to be of any earthly use.

The whole of society is in desperate need of help. It is crying out for someone to give them direction, yet the Church is fast asleep. Look around and see how many of God's servants, who used to be so passionate, zealous and hard-working for God, are now cold, formal and compromising. Many of my brothers that God brought to Britain from Africa with a passion for the lost that was second to none have tasted the garlic, cucumber, hamburgers and the pleasures of the West, and have become desensitized to sin. First they became polarized, then compromised, neutralized, and then finally mesmerized. They have become a shadow of their former selves. Cathedrals that used to be revival centres have now become tourist attractions, places where people pay money to see tombstones and photograph the relics of the men that made Great Britain great!

The whole message of this book is to rouse the sleeping giant.

There's a cry in the Spirit at this hour, it is the cry for the Church of Jesus to wake up from deep slumber. Christ is calling all members of His Body, irrespective of their colour or creed, denomination or theological position to rise up, shake off compromise, shake off lethargy, shake off apathy, shake off indifference, and shake off every weight and the sin that so easily besets us. The night is fast spent, the day is at hand and we must shake off all the works of unrighteousness. We must shake off all forms of carnality and worldliness. The word I hear in the Spirit is even though darkness may cover the land and gross darkness the people, arise, shine for thy light is come and the glory of the Lord is risen upon thee.

> *'Awake, awake, put on strength, O arm of the LORD.'*
>
> (Isaiah 51:9, KJV)

> *'Awake, awake; put on thy strength, O Zion; put on thy beautiful garments, O Jerusalem, the holy city ... Shake thyself from the dust; arise, and sit down, O Jerusalem: loose thyself from the bands of thy neck, O captive daughter of Zion.'*
>
> (Isaiah 52:1–2, KJV)

> *'This is why it is said:*
>
> *"Wake up, O sleeper,*
> *rise from the dead,*
> *and Christ will shine on you."'*
>
> (Ephesians 5:14, NIV)

> *'Awake to righteousness, and do not sin.'*
>
> (1 Corinthians 15:34, NKJV)

> *'And do this, knowing the time, that now it is high time to awake out of sleep.'*
>
> (Romans 13:11a, NKJV)

It is time to rise up and take the land. It is time for us to shine the light of the glorious gospel into all the nooks and crannies of this nation. It is time for a missionary movement to rise out of this land to sweep across Europe and touch the ends of the earth. It is high time to see the glory of God shine in this land again. O Lord, will you rouse Your Church!

> 'Stand up! Stand up for Jesus
> Ye soldiers of the cross
> Lift high his royal banner . . .
> Till every foe is vanquished
> And Christ is Lord indeed.'

(George Duffield)

Put on the gospel armour, each piece put on with prayer

We have identified the situation Jonah was in, in crisis and chaos. We have also seen to our amazement that in the midst of crisis Jonah (the Church) was fast asleep. We have also heard the cry of the Spirit to the Church at this hour – Wake up! As I meditated upon the first six verses of Jonah, I found there was a call to prayer. Notice what the captain said to Jonah: *'Arise, call upon thy God'* (KJV); *'Up, said he, and cry out upon your God!'* (Knox).

This is not another call to a committee meeting. It is a call to prayer. This is the greatest need of the hour. The captain said, 'Up . . . cry out upon God!' This is not just any type of prayer. It is not just a whisper to God. It is not a formal, dead and religious prayer. It is a heartfelt, agonising prayer! It is this kind of prayer that avails much. What does the old English word 'avails' mean? I would like to examine the different Bible versions of James 5:16b to shed light on this:

> *'The effectual fervent prayer of a righteous man availeth much.'*

(KJV)

'The supplication of a righteous man availeth much in its working.'
(ASB)

*'Powerful is **the heartfelt supplication** of a righteous man.'*
(Weymouth, emphasis added)

*'The prayers of the righteous have a **powerful effect**.'*
(Moffat, emphasis added)

*'Tremendous power is made available through a good man's **earnest** prayer.'*
(Phillips, emphasis added)

*'Great is the power of a good man's **fervent** prayer.'*
(TCNT, emphasis added)

*'The prayer of a righteous man **has great power in its effects**.'*
(RSV, emphasis added)

*'When a just man prays **fervently there is great virtue** in his prayer.'*
(Knox, emphasis added)

*'An upright man's prayer, when it **keeps at work** is very powerful.'*
(Wms, emphasis added)

*'The prayer of a righteous man can **bring powerful results**.'*
(Norlie, emphasis added)

*'... makes **tremendous power available** – dynamic in its working.'*
(Amplified, emphasis added)

This is dynamic, persistent, effective prayer, prayer that gets results.

There is so much talk about prayer in the Church today that we have little time left for actually praying. I have been to several 'prayer meetings' for leaders. We strategize, complain about the state of the nation, exchange business cards, have tea breaks and end up doing little or no praying. The curse of this hour is a prayer-less Church.

> 'The pastor who is not praying is playing; the people who are not praying are straying ... Poverty stricken as the Church is today in many things, she is most stricken here, in the place of prayer. We have many organisers but few agonisers; many players and payers, few pray-ers; many singers, few clingers; lots of pastors, few wrestlers; many fears, few tears ... many interferers few intercessors ... Failing here, we fail everywhere.'[8]

Needed in this critical hour are 'pray-ers'.

Elijah, a man of like passions

Elijah appeared at one of the darkest periods in Israel's history. The worship of false gods was everywhere. Israel had one of the most wicked and twisted leaders, Ahab. He was not only a weak and wicked leader, but he had a foreign wife, Jezebel, and allowed her to introduce the worship of Baal, in direct disobedience to God's written instructions. Israel during Ahab's reign was in a period of deep darkness. He not only made a grove, a shrine dedicated to Baal, he promoted Baal worship as the state religion. The Bible says of him he provoked God to anger more than all the previous kings of Israel. It was in the midst of this terrible situation that God raised up the prophet Elijah with no famous ancestry or ministerial qualifications. He was a heaven-sent, God-honouring man that turned Israel back to worship the God of their fathers. How did he achieve this great feat? The record of Scripture is:

> '... *And he repaired the altar of the* LORD *that was broken down.'*
> (1 Kings 18:30b, KJV)

This is the need of this hour. The altar of prayer must be repaired in Christian homes, in our fellowships, and in the cathedrals across this land. For too long the altar of prayer has been neglected and broken. This is the reason for this present darkness.

Sound of abundance of rain

There had been a drought for three and a half years as a sign of God's disapproval of the nation of Israel. After the open defeat of Baal at Carmel, God sent an abundance of rain. After three and a half years of heaven being shut without rain or dew the rain started. This is the need of this nation today, indeed the need of the whole of Europe. We have experienced spiritual drought for decades and we desperately need rain. We need showers of blessing.

Smith Wigglesworth, the apostle of faith, prophesied that in the not too distant future God would send a revival sweeping across this nation which would affect mainland Europe and the rest of the world. I can't wait to see God's glory fill this land again. There shall be showers of blessing; this is the promise of God. There shall be seasons of refreshing, sent from the Father above.

> Showers of blessing
> Showers of blessing we need
> Mercy drops round us are falling
> But for the showers we plead![9]

What was responsible for the outpouring of rain? Let's consider the testimony of the Scriptures:

> '*And Elijah said unto Ahab, Get thee up, eat and drink; for there is a sound of abundance of rain. So Ahab went up to eat and to drink. And Elijah went up to the top of Carmel; and he cast himself down upon the earth, and put his face between his knees. And said to his servant, Go up now, look toward the sea. And he went up, and looked, and said, There is nothing. And he said, Go again seven times. And it came to pass at the seventh time, that he said, Behold, there ariseth a little cloud out of the sea, like a man's hand. And he said, Go up, say unto Ahab, Prepare thy chariot, and get thee down, that the rain stop thee not. And it came to pass in the meanwhile, that the heaven was black with clouds and wind, and there was a great rain. And Ahab rode, and went to Jezreel.'*
> (1 Kings 18:41–45, KJV)

Brothers and sisters I have discovered that nothing just happens. If anything happens, somebody somewhere paid the price. If you see the glory, ask for the story. The point is found in verse 42: '*Elijah went up to the top of Carmel; and he cast himself down upon the earth, and put his face between his knees.*' How can we be sure that when Elijah cast himself down upon the earth, and put his face between his knees he was praying? The book of James validates this claim:

> '[Elijah] *was a man subject to like passions as we are, and he prayed earnestly that it might not rain: and it rained not on the earth by the space of three years and six months. And he prayed again, and the heaven gave rain, and the earth brought her fruit.*'
> (James 5:17–18, KJV)

Elijah was offering deep repentance on behalf of the nation and declaring his strong desire for God to be honoured. This was the

secret to the abundance of rain! This is the secret to all visitations
from heaven. This is the secret of revival. It was not just the
prophetic proclamation that opened heaven. It took prophetic
declaration and heartfelt prayer. This is what I call desperate
prayer, prayer that will not take 'no' for an answer. The scriptures
say, *'he prayed again, and the heaven gave rain'*. Did you notice that
when Elijah made the declaration that abundance of rain was
coming, he told his servant to go and look towards the sea?
Gehazi's response was *'there is nothing'*. I believe this is an
important lesson for all pastors and all prayer and intercessory
ministries. You might not see the immediate manifestation of
your prayers. As we continue to pray, year after year, it might
seem that nothing is shifting. Don't then stop praying. Don't be
discouraged, continue to ask, seek and knock, until your joy is full!

The abundance of rain did not come immediately Elijah made
the declaration; it took continuous, heartfelt, agonising prayers.
This is the kind of prayer that ushers in revival. After all, our Lord
told us that men and women should always 'pray and not lose
heart' (Luke 18:1, RSV).

> *'And He spake a parable unto them to this end, that men ought
> always to pray, and not to faint.'*
>
> (Luke 18:1, KJV)

> *'. . . How necessary it is for people always to pray.'*
>
> (Wms)

> *'And not to be faint-hearted.'*
>
> (Rhm)

> *'And never despair.'*
>
> (TCNT)

> *'And never to give up.'*
>
> (Wms)

Praying for souls

From available statistics we can see that the Church in Britain is in decline. Thousands, if not millions, are going to a Christ-less eternity every year! Most of our altars are empty today, because there are only few people bowing their knees to worship Jesus. Once our Lord saw the pathetic state of souls outside the fold, what was His recommendation to His disciples? Let's read from the Word of God:

> 'But when he saw the multitudes, he was moved with compassion on them, because they fainted, and were scattered abroad, as sheep having no shepherd.
>
> Then saith he unto his disciples, The harvest truly is plenteous, but the labourers are few; **Pray ye therefore the Lord of the harvest, that he will send forth labourers into the harvest.**'
>
> (Matthew 9:36– 38, KJV, emphasis added)

What was Jesus' recommendation to His followers? Prayer, pray ye. You do it. This is the cry of the Spirit today. Pray! While many in the Church today are claiming prosperity as their inheritance, I believe we should be claiming this country.

Suggested practical action

▶ Set aside time each day for prayer for opportunities to share the good news.

▶ Get together with one or more Christians to claim this nation for Christ on a regular basis.

▶ Read through the Bible passages in this chapter in as many versions as possible, meditating on them and declaring the Word of the Lord over the UK.

Wake Up, Esther Church, Your Time Has Come!

'And Mordecai told them to answer Esther: "Do not think in your heart that you will escape in the king's palace any more than all the other Jews. For if you remain completely silent at this time, relief and deliverance will arise for the Jews from another place, but you and your father's house will perish. Yet who knows whether you have come to the kingdom for such a time as this?"'
(Esther 4:13–14, NKJV)

Over the last five years the Lord has been speaking very power-fully to the congregation I pastor and to me from the book of Esther. This led us to adopt as our theme for the prophetic prayer conferences we hold 'For such a time as this'. Many of the things that the Lord has spoken to us I have alluded to in this book in one way or the other, including:

- Identifying the times in which we live.
- Knowing how to respond appropriately.
- Understanding what the devil is trying to do.
- Hearing what the Holy Spirit is doing and saying to the Church.
- The new shape of the Church.
- How to survive in the days ahead.

Since this book is written primarily for the Church in Britain, I will share with you what I believe the Holy Spirit has been speaking to us from the book of Esther.

The book of Esther is the only book that does not mention or use the name of God. In spite of this we can clearly see God at work behind history. I find this very encouraging and extremely relevant to the history of Britain. Sometimes it seems things are so bad we wonder why God allows it. The book of Esther tells us that God is always working behind the scenes. He is in charge of history. Nothing takes Him unawares.

The Christian Life Edition of the New King James Bible gives us a vivid picture of the context of the book. It says:

> 'because of continual disobedience to God over the centuries, particularly in the area of religious compromise, God punished the Jews by allowing them to go into captivity in different nations. However most of them still retain their identity, culture and religion.' [10]

After seventy years of Jewish captivity in Babylon God raised up King Cyrus of Persia who overthrew the kingdom of Babylon. King Cyrus encouraged the Jews to return to their homeland and rebuild the temple. In the year 536 BC fifty thousand Jews returned to Jerusalem under the leadership of Zerubbabel the governor and Jeshua the high priest. Ezra and Nehemiah, the two Old Testament books preceding the book of Esther, tell the story of the Jews who returned to their homeland. The majority of Jews in Persia and Babylon, however, preferred to stay living comfortably under the Persians.

God chooses Esther

The book of Esther begins by telling us how king Ahasuerus deposed his wife, Queen Vashti, for refusing to appear at his banquet. That left the position of queen vacant and a process was set in motion to select a new queen. Through the sovereign hand of God Esther, cousin of Mordecai the Jew, was chosen.

> *'For not from the east nor from the west nor from the south come promotion and lifting up. But God is the judge! He puts down one, and lifts up another.'*
>
> (Psalm 75:6–7, Amplified)

> *'Every good and every perfect gift is from above, and cometh down from the Father of lights, with whom is no variableness, neither shadow of turning.'*
>
> (James 1:17, KJV)

> *'John answered and said, A man can receive nothing, except it be given him from heaven.'*
>
> (John 3:27, KJV)

You might be tempted out of ignorance to think the appointment of Esther in place of Vashti was a coincidence, but I know from my knowledge of Scripture that nothing is a coincidence. Promotion only comes from one place, from above. God is the one who chooses who rules a nation. The heart of the king is in His hands, and He can turn it wherever He desires. The selection of Esther did not happen by chance. I love to say it is a God-incidence! It was the work of the One who inhabits eternity, whose name is Elohim. Who else could have brought Esther to the throne? To begin with she was not qualified because she was a foreigner. This was why her identity was concealed for a long time. In spite of that, throughout the selection process Esther received unusual favour. She received beauty preparation well above most of the others. Let's see the scriptures:

> *'Now the young woman pleased him, and she obtained his favour; so he readily gave beauty preparations to her, besides her allowance. Then seven choice maidservants were provided for her from the king's palace, and he moved her and her maidservants to the best place in the house of the women.'*
>
> (Esther 2:9, NKJV)

Take note of this, Esther enjoyed unusual favour. She got the best place. Favour comes only from God. I searched my Bible and I discovered that we can receive favour from both God and man. When God wants to bless, promote or honour a person or a nation, He grants them favour.

- God gave Nehemiah favour before the king (Nehemiah 2:5)
- God brought Daniel into favour (Daniel 1:9)
- Mary received favour from God and thus became the mother of Jesus (Luke 1:30)
- Jesus Himself received favour from God and man (Luke 2:52)
- The early Church obtained favour with all the people (Acts 2:47)

Let's be quite clear about this, God is the only giver of favour. Esther received favour from God, not because of who she was, or her qualifications, but because of the mercy, grace and the plan of God. You too receive favour from God because He loves you and wants the best for you, not because you have done anything outstanding to earn it.

> *'Now when the turn came for Esther the daughter of Abihail the uncle of Mordecai, who had taken her as his daughter, to go into the king, she requested nothing but what Hegai the king's eunuch, the custodian of the women, advised. **And Esther obtained favour in the sight of all who saw her.**'*
>
> (Esther 2:15, NKJV, emphasis added)

Esther did not just obtain favour from one, two or even five people; she enjoyed favour from everyone who saw her. This is nothing other than a miracle.

Whatever God does is for a reason and it is for a season. God is a God of purpose. God does not make mistakes. He has a purpose and a time for everything. If God plants you somewhere – college, business, city, nation – it is for a reason and for a season! If God plants you in Manchester and not Munich, Leeds rather than Lagos, it is for a reason and for a season. There's no accident in God. So we must always endeavour to find out what is God's, plan and assignment for us in our place of planting.

It was God who planted Esther in her location, to be there at a specific moment and for a strategic purpose. No wonder one of the most quoted, and most remembered verses in the book of Esther is *'for such a time as this'* (Esther 4:14, KJV).

The enemy hatches a plot

Chapter 3 of the book of Esther tells us about the plan of Haman to destroy the Jews throughout the kingdom on a fixed date. Anti-Semitism is not a new thing. The devil has always incited people throughout the generations to destroy the Jews. God still upholds the covenant that He made with the patriarchs in spite of the fact that many of the Jews have turned their backs on their Messiah.

God is still faithful to His covenant. He will make sure that the schemes of the enemy, the devil, come to nought. Let the modern-day Haman pay attention:

> *'Behold they shall surely gather together, but not by me: whosoever shall gather together against thee shall fall for thy sake.'*
>
> (Isaiah 54:15, KJV)

Haman paid large sums of money, ten thousand talents of silver, into the king's treasury in order to destroy the Jews. Some have estimated that to be worth around $3.84 billion today. The enemy will go to almost any lengths to destroy God's heritage. Haman's skill got the king to pass a decree, signed and sealed, so that it could not be revoked.

> *'And the letters were sent by couriers into all the king's provinces, to destroy, to kill, and to annihilate all the Jews, both young and old, little children and women, in one day, on the thirteenth day of the twelfth month, which is the month of Adar, and to plunder their possessions. A copy of the document was to be issued as law in every province, being published for all people, that they should be ready for that day. The couriers went out, hastened by the king's command; and the decree was proclaimed in Shushan the citadel. So the king and Haman sat down to drink, but the city of Shushan was perplexed.'*
>
> (Esther 3:13–15, NKJV)

This was a strategic plot by the enemy!

A message for the Church in Britain

I believe this nation is at a pivotal moment of history. There is a well thought out plan by the enemy to destroy the Judeo-Christian heritage that this nation has enjoyed for many centuries.

On 26 December 2004 *The Times* reported, 'Charles plans his modern coronation'. The article reads:

> 'The royal family has started making preparations for the Prince of Wales to become king by secretly devising sweeping changes to modernise the coronation and other ceremonies marking his accession. Under the review courtiers are considering pruning "puritanical" elements of the coronation ceremony and creating a new role for leaders of the non-Christian religions in the service.' [11]

The coronation of Charles is expected to be a multi-faith service. This will depart from centuries of British tradition, and require major changes dividing Church and state that at present is legally united. This will not come as a surprise to many, since the heir apparent has hinted in the past that he wants to change one of his titles from 'defender of the faith' to become the 'defender of faiths'. This also will need a change to the present situation where the ruling monarch is also head of the Church of England. I wonder if anyone is putting the prince under pressure to make these changes, if the Muslims, Hindus or Sikhs are asking for a change. I wonder whether the people of nations such as Saudi Arabia or Iran would ever consider giving those of non-Muslim religious faiths the same religious freedom. I love people of other faiths and believe they should be allowed religious freedom, but I also believe the heir apparent should be speaking out more about the injustice that Christians are suffering in many nations that are closed to the gospel.

There is a conspiracy to destroy the institution of the family as we have known it for many generations. There is a plot to corrupt our children with violent and pornographic films. There's a plot to limit our right of expression. There's a plot to stop us from declaring that Jesus is the only way to God. This is all a modern-day conspiracy of Haman!

God has a plan too

God is never taken unawares. It doesn't matter how dark the situation looks, it doesn't matter if the devil has a plot, it doesn't matter how terrible things seem at the moment, God is still in charge. He is in control. He is not short of ideas or strategies. God's strategies may not be too clear to us. God's instruments may not be known by mortal man, yet God is still in control. Pastors and Church leaders relax, be confident in this. God will have the final say regarding this nation! Even though Haman had his plans, so also did God.

God often uses the most unusual persons, the lowly, the insignificant, the despised, rejected, the unqualified and the weak to carry out His plans.

> *'For you see your calling, brethren, that not many wise according to the flesh, not many mighty, not many noble, are called. But God has chosen the foolish things of the world to put to shame the wise, and God has chosen the weak things of the world to put to shame the things which are mighty; and the base things of the world and the things which are despised God has chosen, and the things which are not, to bring to nothing the things which are, that no flesh should glory in His presence.'*
>
> (1 Corinthians 1:26–29, NKJV)

The instruments of God's glory and power will be nobodies. They will be insignificant people who have been despised and rejected by men, men and women who are in obscurity, men and women of no renowned family background. The days of the superstars are over.

Esther, an insignificant unqualified person for the throne, was planted at a strategic location, the palace, for a strategic hour. This is what I call the Esther Church. The Church of today has been raised by God and positioned for this strategic moment! Even though there's a spiritual conspiracy, God has strategically positioned a remnant. They are nameless and faceless, with no ministerial title attached to their names. They don't belong to the big circle of ministers. Their names have never been seen or heard in the media. They are the Elijahs of this hour. They are destiny carriers and nation changers! Many of them have their training not in cathedrals, not in palaces of stained glass, but in the wilderness! They have been waxing strong in the Spirit until the day of their showing.

Esther, it's time to wake up

The stage is now set for the extinction of the Jews. The plot has been signed and sealed. Where would deliverance come from? Who has God prepared for this hour and how will they know? God raised up Mordecai, a fearless man, a man who would not bow to the scheme of wicked, satanically inspired Haman. Mordecai sent a copy of the decree to Esther, to show her Haman's plot and to request her to go before the king to plead on behalf of her people, even though she knew she must not speak or approach the king without his permission. Indeed it was taking an enormous risk going to the king unless she had been sent for. She knew what had happened to her predecessor! It was against the law for anyone to approach the king unless he sent for them. If they went anyway, unless he held out his sceptre to them and invited them to speak, they would be put to death.

Esther had not been sent for for the past thirty days! What was she to do? Was she going to risk her life or keep quiet? Was she going to take a risk or allow the devil to continue his rampage? Will the Esther Church rise up in a nation where the name of our Lord is being desecrated? Will the Esther Church rise up and contend for the truth, even though it is not politically correct? Will the Esther Church rise up like little David and face Goliath, or are we going to go into hiding?

Esther's response

'Then Esther spoke to Hathach, and gave him a command for Mordecai: "All the king's servants and the people of the king's provinces know that any man or woman who goes into the inner court to the king, who has not been called, he has but one law: put all to death, except the one to whom the king holds out the golden sceptre, that he may live. Yet I myself have not been called to go in to the king these thirty days." '

(Esther 4:10–11, NKJV)

Excuses! Excuses! Excuses! Esther was simply giving excuses! This is what I see and hear in the Church today! There's great danger today in Britain if you preach the unadulterated Word of God. You will be called a fundamentalist, homophobic, Islamophobic, politically incorrect and you could even lose your job, friends, family and freedom for preaching deemed to be inciting racial hatred, all for being faithful to what you believe to be the Word of God.

Anyone who contends for the faith in these days might end up in prison. It is a real possibility. I believe we need to be wise and humble, but there's no place in Scripture where we are told to compromise our faith. Esther had forgotten how she came to the throne. She had totally forgotten that she was not qualified to be in the palace. She had totally forgotten that it was not her background, education or beauty that brought her to the strategic position. It was not her eloquence or anything about her. It was all the finger of God. Esther had forgotten that her planting was of God for a strategic assignment. She was God's instrument of deliverance at a strategic moment.

Esther needed to be woken up to this reality. Esther needed to be confronted with reality and divine purpose. It took Mordecai to wake Esther up to her divine assignment and calling. Oh how we need this ministry of Mordecai in this moment of compromise in our nation! Only the Holy Spirit can wake up the Church that is fast asleep!

Listen to a word of advice from Africa

I want to thank God for the great work that He is doing in Britain at the moment through my brothers and sisters from the continent of Africa. Without mincing words, I believe the spiritual landscape of Britain would be very different today without the input of people from Africa and the Caribbean. I want to acknowledge the great work being done by all those that God has brought from different parts of the world for this hour of great need in Britain, from South America, Asia, Europe, the Middle East and elsewhere. I salute you for your perseverance, sacrifice, prayers and your labour of love to the cause of Christ in Great Britain. Be assured the spiritual history of this nation in the late twentieth and early twenty-first centuries would be incomplete without you! Also be assured that your reward is reserved for you in heaven. However, because my family came from Africa I believe I can say that some of the folk from Africa are asleep. They have fallen into a state of spiritual slumber. Many came into this nation with great zeal and fire, with a vision and passion for revival. I have heard again and again brothers and sisters tell me, when they first came here, they were convinced that God sent them on a divine assignment. God sent them here to be a part of the revival that is coming. But if you look more closely you will discover that many have fallen into a similar state that Israel fell into when they settled down in the Promised Land. Let's read the warning that God gave them as they were about to possess the land of Canaan:

> 'So it shall be, when the LORD your God brings you into the land of which He swore to your fathers, to Abraham, Isaac, and Jacob, to

give you large and beautiful cities which you did not build, houses
full of all good things, which you did not fill, hewn-out wells which
you did not dig, vineyards and olive trees which you did not plant
– when you have eaten and are full – then beware, lest you forget
the LORD who brought you out of the land of Egypt, from the house
of bondage.'

(Deuteronomy 6:10–12, NKJV)

God warned them to be careful, because where they were going they would come into many good things, beautiful clothes, abundant food, amusement parks, a lot of places to enjoy pleasures. He warned them to be very careful not to be overtaken by the deceitfulness of riches, by the rich food in the land, by the prospects of making **big** money! He warned them to be careful about avoiding the worship of the gods of the people already living in the land. They should avoid the religion of the indigenous people already settled there. After all, it was because of their idolatry that the Children of Israel were told not to follow their practices. What do we find? Mammon! He warned them that it would be folly for them to forget Him once they got to this land.

For those of us who know the plot, this was exactly what happened. Israel became engrossed in the land; they began to worship the gods of the land and forgot Yahweh. This is exactly what I see happening in many of my brothers and sisters that have been sent here on a divine mission. Many pastors have abandoned their call in order to make a few pounds. This is exactly what I see happening to many.

Many of my brothers and sisters on getting to the 'promised land' have ceased going for fellowship, stopped giving to the cause of Christ, are not rooted and established in a local fellowship, and no longer have the passion for souls that they used to have. Fasting has become a thing of the past. Many people are sound asleep in the lap of Delilah. Many pastors will tell you that some of their greatest headaches are their 'brothers' and 'sisters', those that professed Christ before they came to Britain but show little evidence of their faith now that they are here. Great Britain, for many believers from Africa, is a graveyard where many mighty men and women have been buried spiritually. Mind you, they still expect you to follow them up and remind them about services every week. What a shame. What a disappointment many of us have become to God. The Word of the Lord to you today is it's time you woke up from your slumber. It's time you woke up to reality. It's time to pick up your God-given assignment that you dropped some years ago. It's time to get serious for the King. It's time to go into the highways, and the byways and compel men to come in! It's time to reap the harvest of the nation, for the field is white for harvest! It's time to get serious again!

My brothers and sisters from the continent of Africa are not the only ones sound asleep; the same spirit affects many that God has sent from the Caribbean. Many have become distracted and side-tracked. What about the situation of the churches generally? We are by and large in a state of slumber. We are indifferent to what is happening around us. We are somewhat indifferent to what is happening in politics, media, in education and on our streets. It's time for the Esther Church to arise and shine for our light has come and the glory of the Lord is risen upon us. Thank God for Mordecai, God's instrument to wake up the dozing Esther Church. God is once again raising up prophetic voices calling the Esther Church to rise up! Wake up! Stand up!

I am reminded of the song of one of our great songwriters Graham Kendrick:

> 'Darkness like a shroud covers the earth,
> Evil like a cloud covers the people
> But the Lord will rise upon you,
> And His glory will appear on you
> Nations will come to your light.

Arise shine; your light is come,
The glory of the Lord has risen on you!
Arise, shine, your light has come,
Jesus the light of the world has come.

Children of the light, be clean and pure.
Rise, you sleepers, Christ will shine on you.
Take the Spirit's flashing two-edged sword
And with faith declare God's mighty Word,
Stand up and in His strength be strong.

Here among us now,
Christ the light kindles brighter flames in our
      trembling hearts
Living word, our lamp, come guide our feet
As we walk as one in light and peace,
Till justice and truth shine like the sun.
Like a city bright so let us blaze,
Lights in every street turning night to day.
And the darkness shall not overcome
Till the fullness of Christ's kingdom comes,
Dawning to God's eternal day.' [12]

When the Esther Church wakes up

After Mordecai's challenge to Esther to take up her calling and
destiny, she took several steps that are instructive to the Church
today.

> 'Then Esther told them to reply to Mordecai: "Go, gather all the
> Jews who are present in Shushan, and fast for me; neither eat nor
> drink for three days, night or day. My maids and I will fast
> likewise. And so I will go to the king, which is against the law; and
> if I perish, I perish!" '
>
> (Esther 4:15–16, NKJV)

The first thing I want to point out is that Esther took a risk. She risked her life! She went before the king without being invited. This might well have led to her death. Didn't Jesus say to us that if we lose our life for His sake, we shall find it?

Revelation 12:11 says:

> *'And they overcame him by the blood of the Lamb and by the word of their testimony, and they did not love their lives to the death.'*
>
> (NKJV)

The Esther Church must take risks, even if it means laying down their lives. The blood of the martyrs has always been the seed of the Church. The Church has always thrived in the midst of persecution. Many missionaries from this nation laid down their lives, so that many of us might hear the gospel. It's time for us to do likewise.

Secondly, Esther called three days of fasting in order to go and petition the king. She knew that the situation at stake was a serious one. It was a desperate situation. A desperate situation demands a desperate solution. This is what we need in Britain. It does not seem to me that the Church understands the enormity of the situation we are facing. Rather, to turn it around we have refused to acknowledge the situation. Note again what Esther did, she called for a desperate fast. No food for three whole days. How I wish Church leaders would take their cue from this. How I wish the Anglicans, Baptists, Catholics, Presbyterians, Methodists, Charismatics, Pentecostals and all who name the name of the Lord would admit that there is a serious and desperate situation confronting the Church and the nation today. How I wish we would declare a national day or days of repentance, consecration and prayer so that we can go before the King to plead for the Church and the nation so that He can spare us further judgment. It's time to wake up. This is the season for prayer for our children, for the media, for our educational system, for the Church. The whole issue of Europe should be taken before the Lord in prayer and fasting. We should take the issue of Britain's relationship with Israel to God in prayer. It's time we took ourselves before the Lord in prayer and fasting for the multitude of people dying everyday to a Christ-less eternity. It's time to pray.

It was done in Uganda

Most of you are aware of what the nation of Uganda used to be. After many years under despotic and tyrannical leaders when many people were killed, including an archbishop, the nation's treasury was looted, and there was also total sabotage of the nation's infrastructure. Hospitals had no supplies, people went without running water or electricity, even in the capital, Kampala. Worst of all, the nation was seriously plagued by the AIDS epidemic. Whole families and villages were being wiped out. In this pathetic state, the Church became desperate. The Church leaders knew that it would take a supernatural intervention to transform their nation. How did the Church in Uganda respond?

They began to hold days, weeks and months of prayer and fasting meetings. They became so desperate that many leaders would spend several weeks in the woods without food seeking the Lord in prayer for a change in their nation. Catholics, Anglicans, Charismatics and Orthodox believers started praying together in the north. The effect is what we see today. Many churches held all-night prayer meetings regularly and still continue to this day. Massive church growth and transformation of cities is happening. Christian radio and TV stations are mushrooming. While the number of AIDS victims is rising at an alarming rate in many parts of Africa, it is actually reported that the number of new cases is going down in Uganda. Thanks to the risk that the Church took in Uganda this has led to the transformation of their nation. The Christian leaders in Uganda must have taken a cue from Esther; they were so desperate for change that they were ready to lay down their lives for this worthy cause. This is what the Holy Spirit is calling us into in Great Britain. It has happened in Cali in Columbia! Whole cities transformed by God through the prayers of the church. After watching the *Transformations* video, my heart pants to God to see the same thing happening here.

Suggested practical action

▶ Pray that every conspiracy of our enemy, Satan, in our nation like that of Haman is brought to nought.

▶ Pray that God wakes up the Church so we can see the schemes of the enemy to destroy our Judaeo-Christian values and also know how to respond appropriately.

▶ Pray for reformers to become active in this land; godly men and women like Elizabeth Fry, John Howard and William Wilberforce, and organizations such as the Clapham Sect.

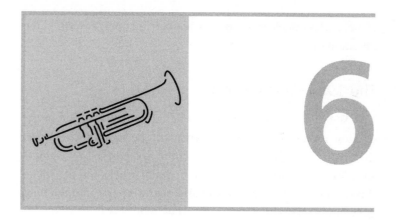

Lessons from History

'So it shall be, when the LORD your God brings you into the land ...
beware, lest you forget the LORD who brought you out of the land
of Egypt.'
(Deuteronomy 6:10a, 12b, NKJV)

The study of history has always been a profitable venture. History informs us about the past, what happened, the reasons why things happened. It also informs us about important personalities, why they became important or changed the course of history. History serves to inspire us, to encourage us, to make us understand that history makers are not superhuman. It challenges us to do what they did so that we can get the results that they got. I am always inspired, provoked and challenged when I read the history of revivals. Since most of us are believing God for a change in the spiritual climate of Britain and Europe, it will be a worthwhile exercise to do some research into our history to see why revival came, and particularly to look at the part that prayer took in the initiation of revival.

The 1904 Welsh revival

The Welsh revival of 1904 is considered by many as one of the greatest modern-day revivals particularly because of the impact that it left on Welsh society. The central figure in this revival was Evan Roberts, born in 1878. Without doubt prayer was the key to this revival. On his prayer life, Evan Roberts reports after the Lord gave him a vision:

> 'I was frightened that night, but never since. So great was my shivering that I rocked the bed. My brother Dan, being awakened, took hold of me thinking I was ill. After that experience I was awakened every night at one o'clock. From that time I was taken up into divine fellowship. About five o'clock I was allowed to sleep until nine. It was too divine to say anything about. I cannot describe it but I felt it. It changed my whole nature.' [13]

Evan Roberts was a man who had a heavy burden for the state of things in Wales, particularly the pathetic state of the Church. This is a lesson we must learn today, if we are going to change the spiritual climate of this nation. We must carry a serious burden, which must be translated into prayer. On Evan's burden and prayer for Wales, Brynmor Pierce Jones quotes Evan Roberts:

> 'I was troubled in my soul by thinking of the failure of Christianity. Such a failure. I prayed and prayed but nothing seemed to give me any relief. One night, after I had been in great distress praying about this, I went to sleep. At nine o'clock I was awakened out of my sleep and found myself with unspeakable joy and awe, in the very presence of

Almighty God. For the space of four hours I was privileged
to speak with Him as a man speaks with his friend. I saw
things in a different light. I knew God was going to work in
the land.' [14]

When and where did this prayer work begin? D.M. Philips said
that the potential was there long before the revival. Speaking
about Roberts' prayer life he states: 'when most intense in prayer,
he becomes unconscious of everything else. Time for him does
not exist. Hours glide away in a moment. He is insensible of all
that happens'.[15]

Evan Roberts was so taken up with the idea of vigilant
watching that he prayed night and day and was even known to
fall asleep on his feet, then awaken a few hours later fresh and
alert once more. This was how much given to prayer he was. Is it
therefore a coincidence that God sent revival to Wales? I don't
think so. Like Evan Roberts, God is looking for people, men and
women, who will not give Him rest until He sends the rain of
revival to our land. Remember God has not changed His
principles. He said through the prophets of old:

'And I sought for a man among them, that should make up the
hedge, and stand in the gap before me for the land . . . '

(Ezekiel 22:30, KJV)

The Welsh revival of 1735

Wales has been rightly described as the Land of Revivals.
Although John Wesley and George Whitefield are the two best
known names of the eighteenth-century revival, they were not
the only ones God used. There were men God used very
powerfully in Wales before them. What was the state of things
in Wales? Who were the instruments of this revival and what can

we learn about the place of prayer in this revival? On the state of things before the revival, Colin Whittaker remarks:

> 'Following the restoration of Charles II, Wales had declined politically and spiritually. There was in fact a revival of the wrong sort – an upsurge of the occult and the renewed practise of divination and black magic.' [16]

Swearing, lying, drunkenness, fighting and gambling were the order of the day. Howell Harris was one of the principal instruments of the revival. After his conversion at the age of twenty-one, he immediately gave himself to testifying about the risen Lord and to much prayer. His biographer, Richard Bennett, comments on his prayer life: 'in the secret place with his God, Harris was in his element. Soon after his conversion, as he prayed alone for hours in the church tower of the village where he was then teaching, God met him in power'.[17] So powerful was Harris' ministry that he not only converted several people into the kingdom of God, but he set the Welsh revival in progress, which virtually ended the cruel sports and the promiscuous festivals of the time and many people's behaviour changed dramatically.

The other personality that God used tremendously in the Welsh revival was Daniel Rowland, a man who came to faith through the earnest prayer and ministry of Griffith Jones, who has been called the morning star of the revival. So successful was his ministry that on Sundays he often had between two thousand and two thousand five hundred communicants. People also travelled as far as fifty or sixty miles to come and hear him. Remember, this was in the days when you walked, or rode if you were wealthy, which most Welsh people were not. Nowadays the same journey might take just over an hour by car, but it would take about ten hours to walk that distance.

So what was the secret to the success of this man's ministry and indeed the revival? Let's look again to Colin Whittaker to give us this vital information. He writes:

'As well as a great preacher, he was a great man of prayer. He often went to the top of the Aeron Hills to pour out his heart to God in fervent prayer and for the salvation of the people in the region. It was said by those who knew him that he lived in the spirit of prayer and that this was a great secret of his success. On one occasion he was due to preach at a church, which was on a hilltop; he had to cross a valley in sight of the people who were waiting for him in the churchyard. They saw him descend into the valley out of sight for a little while. They waited, expecting him to appear again as soon as he ascended from the valley but the time came for the service to commence and he had still not appeared. Some went to search for him and they discovered him on knees in a sheltered spot. He got up as soon as he saw them and went with them, expressing regret for the delay, but he added, "I had a delightful opportunity below." The sermon which followed was attended by extra-ordinary power.'[18]

Here was the secret to the Welsh revivals. Here is the secret of any revival. God is not prodigal with His power. If we will pay the price in our generation, God will pour out His Spirit upon us and upon our land – Great Britain, but He is waiting for us to ask, seek and knock. Will any one respond?

The Hebrides revival of 1949

Since this book is primarily a call to the nation of Great Britain, it would be helpful to see what God did in the past in Scotland. The man at the centre of the Hebrides revival was Duncan Campbell of the Faith Mission. The key characteristic of this revival was the overwhelming sense of the presence of God. His sacred presence was everywhere and sinners found it impossible to escape it! This is the great need of today! But how did this come about? It was prayer and much prayer.

Many people were praying. Peggy Smith, an eighty-four-year-old woman who was blind, and her sister Christine who was afflicted with serious arthritis, were key prayer warriors for the revival. God uses women! God uses weak vessels too and indeed He uses the most unlikely candidates. Those two sisters in the early hours of a winter morning in 1949, in a little cottage near Barvas village on the isle of Lewis, were in serious and earnest prayer to God. It was at this prayer meeting that God met with them in a very special way giving them an unmistakable assurance that the revival that they and many others had been praying for was very near. What happened next should be a lesson for all believers, particularly church leaders. This should act as a challenge and inspiration to all of us across the British Isles to take prayer more seriously. Peggy sent for her minister James Murray-Mackay after God visited her and shared what she believed was a revelation from God. She further challenged her pastor to call the church leaders to prayer. The pastor responded positively.

> 'This man of God responded and for months, three nights a week, he and others met to do business with Almighty God in real prayer.' [19]

They prayed for several months three nights a week. This is the key. Are we serious with God? Are we desperate for revival? Do we want to see our cities consumed with the presence of God? Do we want to see God's glory in this land again? If so there's a price to pay. It might mean cancelling our regular programmes, emptying our diaries, and doing business with God in the place of prayer. Are we desperate enough? I believe the saints experienced the Hebrides revival because they were desperate. This is the only reason people would pray for months three times a week.

God used old Peggy in a powerful way because she was a woman of prayer. In fact God often used her in channelling the direction and the instruments of the revival. For example, Rev. Mackay felt led to invite Duncan Campbell to Barvas for special meetings. This leading was endorsed by Peggy because God had revealed to her in a vision that the instrument He was going to use would be Duncan Campbell. Mr Campbell received a telegram inviting him to come to Lewis. Naturally speaking it was impossible because he was already busy preaching fruitfully on Skye, another island. His response was that he would put Lewis on his agenda for next year. When the two praying sisters heard this, their response simply was, 'That is what man has said. God has said "He is coming, and he will be here within the fortnight."'[20] Duncan Campbell related, 'I cannot go into details as to how it was necessary to cancel the convention. All I can say is that Peggy's prayer was answered and within a fortnight I was there.'[21]

England 1739 – the great awakening

What was the state of England before the great awakening? According to all records it was very similar to the situation we are in today. Morally and spiritually England was at a low ebb. England was morally and spiritually bankrupt. The rot at this time had not only affected the man on the street but also the man on the throne. The monarch of the day had irregular liaisons with many women. This rot had also affected the Church. Our literature, art, theatre and culture were so corrupt that they shocked even the most hardened visitors from abroad. The theatre was shockingly vulgar and depraved. Drunkenness made the very name of Englishmen stink in the nostrils of other nations. Polygamy, homosexuality and fornication were hardly considered sinful! In many respects England in the 1730s was exactly where we are today. It seems to me from what I read in the papers that we are simply repeating history. What was the Church doing before 1739? For most part exactly what we are doing today, sleeping soundly. Bishop Ryle says:

> 'Both Anglican and non-conformists seemed at least agreed on one point – and that was to let the devil alone and to do nothing for hearts and souls.' [22]

Such was the state of the nation and the Church that England could be described as a nation that was ripe for judgment. Amazingly, rather than judgment, God showed mercy! This is the same mercy that I am praying for today. God took hold of two men, George Whitefield and John Wesley, and used them as instruments of His to turn the course of history. We cannot fully write the history of the great awakening, particularly the contributions of Wesley, without mention being made of the impact that the Moravians had on him. In the summer of 1738 Wesley spent three months in Germany visiting the Moravians in Herrnhut, under the leadership of Count Nicolaus Zinzendorf. In 1727 the Moravian community experienced a powerful awakening. The highlight was a community service, which signalled the coming of the Holy Spirit. The consequence was that a fire for world missions was ignited in the hearts of those Moravians. This started what has been described as the longest prayer meeting since the birth of the Church. The young cleric John Wesley met some of them on a sea journey to America that drove him to seek an impartation from God through them. He returned to England greatly strengthened and encouraged. Thus the fire for revival was passed to John Wesley by the Moravians.

On 1 January 1739 the Wesleys, Charles and John, George Whitefield and four others from their 'holy club' (a gathering of like-minded ordinands to promote the leading of a sanctified life), with some sixty others, met in London for prayer and a love feast. I want you to notice the significance of prayer. So powerful was the visitation of the Spirit of God upon these praying saints that many of them were so overwhelmed that the meeting continued all night long. We can know this first hand from the biography of John Wesley:

> 'Mr Hall, Kinchin, Ingham, Whitefield, Hitchins, and my brother Charles were at our love feast in Fetter Lane, with about sixty of our brethren. About three in the morning, as we were continuing instant in prayer, the power of God came mightily upon us, insomuch that many cried out for exceeding joy, and many fell to the ground. As soon as we were recovered a little from that awe and amazement at the presence of his majesty, we broke out with one voice, we praise Thee, O God, we acknowledge Thee to be the Lord.' [23]

This outpouring of the Spirit marked the beginning of the evangelical revival that transformed every sphere of life in Great Britain. Rather than revolution as experienced by France, we experienced revival because some people gave themselves to prayer. No-one can deny the fact that Great Britain truly became great as a result of the evangelical revival. Today there are clouds of darkness all over our nation. They cover politics, media, education, business and indeed the Church. Nothing short of this kind of revival will do in this desperate hour. The scriptural injunction in 2 Chronicles 7:14 is still true today. There is a big condition attached to this scripture:

> *'If My people ... will humble themselves, and pray and seek My face, and turn from their wicked ways, then I will hear from heaven, and will forgive their sin and heal their land.'*
>
> (2 Chronicles 7:14, NKJV)

Only if we fulfil the conditions can we experience forgiveness and the healing of our land. May God bring us to our knees.

Suggested practical action

▶ Read books on revivals. This will inform and inspire us to believe for revival in our land. I highly recommend John Pollock's *Wesley the Preacher: A Biography* (Kingsway Books), Colin Whittaker's *Great Revivals* (Marshalls) and Leonard Ravenhill's *Why Revival Tarries* (Bethany Books).

▶ Research prophetic words such as those given by Smith Wigglesworth, Evan Roberts and others.

▶ Link up with ministries and individuals that carry a revival anointing, such as www.heartcry.co.uk, www.renewalcc.com, www.Gloryhouse.org.uk

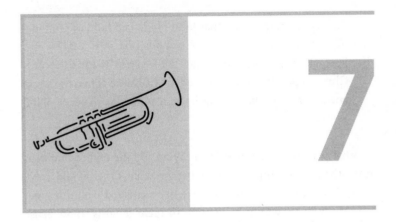

Adding Souls to the Kingdom

'Ask of me, and I shall give thee the heathen for thine inheritance, and the uttermost parts of the earth for thy possession.'
(Psalm 2:8, KJV)

The Church should claim the whole of the British Isles, England, Scotland, Ireland and Wales for the Lord. The will of God is that no-one should perish. When believers pray specifically and boldly people are born into the kingdom of God. This was the burden for souls that John, 'Praying Hyde', had. This apostle of prayer would plead with God night and day for souls with sobs and tears – 'Father give me these souls, or I die!' was the burden of his prayers.

One soul a day

In 1908 John Hyde, known as 'Praying Hyde', began to ask God for a soul a day. Captain E.G. Carre writes about John's burden for a soul a day:

'It was about this time that John Hyde laid hold of God in a very definite covenant. This was for one soul a day – not less, not inquirers simply, but a soul saved – ready to confess Christ in public and be baptised in His Name. Then the stress and strain was relieved. His heart was filled with peace of full assurance.' [24]

What was the outcome of his praying? By the end of that year more than four hundred were gathered in. One would have thought that John Hyde would have been satisfied with this great feat. Many of us would have gone to great lengths to advertise our success, not Mr Hyde. In his mind he kept hearing his Master say, 'Other sheep I have – other sheep I have.' By 1909 John had again laid hold of God with a definite and importunate request. This time it was for two souls a day. As I read the prayers of John Hyde for souls, I really feel ashamed and provoked at the same time:

'Lord, give me thy heart of love for sinners, thy broken heart for their sins, thy tears with which to admonish night and day. But, O Lord, I feel so cold. My heart is so hard and dead. I am so lukewarm!' [25]

By 1910 John Hyde had laid hold on God again in holy desperation. By this time his prayer was, 'Give me four souls a day or I die.' This is the need of this hour. This is what we need in this nation, an army of intercessors who will 'plunder hell and populate heaven'! [26]

Lessons from the early Church

Once I began to ask the Lord why the early Church grew the way it did. Why did it experience the supernatural the way it did? Why did the gospel spread fast and wide to foreign lands? Why was it that the gates of hell could not prevail against the early Church in spite of all the attacks? The answer was simply the praying Church. The Lord challenged me to study the early Church to see the place they gave to prayer. My findings were rewarding and inspiring.

The Church was born in prayer (Acts 1:4–5)

Before Jesus was taken up into heaven, He charged His disciples not to leave Jerusalem but to wait for the promise of the Holy Spirit. In other words they were not to do anything and preach no message without the power of the Holy Spirit coming upon them.

> *'Do not leave Jerusalem, but wait for the gift my Father promised, which you have heard me speak about. For John baptised with water, but in a few days you will be baptised with the Holy Spirit.'*
> (Acts 1:4b–5, NIV)

After the ascension what did the disciples do?

> *'Then they returned to Jerusalem from the hill called the Mount of Olives, a Sabbath day's walk from the city. When they arrived, they went upstairs to the room where they were staying. Those present were Peter, John, James and Andrew; Philip and Thomas, Bartholomew and Matthew; James son of Alphaeus and Simon the Zealot, and Judas son of James.* **They all joined together constantly in prayer,** *along with the women and Mary the mother of Jesus, and with his brothers.'*
> (Acts 1:12–14, NIV, emphasis added)

Take note what they were doing – they all joined together constantly in prayer. They did not go to a committee meeting, no! They went to wait and pray for the Holy Spirit's power. This is our great need for today. Without this the Church will continue to be cold, sick and anaemic. It was while they were waiting and praying that the Holy Spirit came like a mighty rushing wind and the Church was born! The Church was born in a prayer meeting. A friend of mine once told me that whatever gave birth to you, you need it to survive. As humans, blood and water were crucial at our birth, therefore we need them to survive. As the Church of Jesus we were born in prayer; without a doubt we will need prayer to survive.

In Acts 2:42 we see the regular routine of the church – teaching, fellowship, breaking of bread and prayer.

> '*They devoted themselves to the apostles' teaching and to the fellowship, to the breaking of bread and to prayer.*'
>
> (NIV)

A cripple healed at the hour of prayer (Acts 3:1–16)

The first recorded miracle in the early Church was when a man that had been lame for over forty years was healed. This had the effect of not only bringing praise and honour to God, but also it gave further opportunity for the preaching of the gospel to the unbelievers, who were bewildered at the miracle. One important thing that struck me was that the miracle occurred at the hour of prayer.

> '*One day Peter and John were going up to the temple at the time of prayer – at three in the afternoon.*'
>
> (Acts 3:1, NIV)

The early Church experienced phenomenal miracles because they dedicated times to pray regularly. Are we hungry for the miraculous? Do we want to see the lame walk, the blind see? If this is our desire, we must follow the example of the early Church.

The early Church and persecution (Acts 4:23–31)

The healing of the lame man put the disciples on a collision course with the religious elite of the day. They ordered the disciples to stop preaching in the name of Jesus, because the miracle had the effect of drawing people to Christ! What an irony, the leaders of God's people trying to prevent them coming to relationship with Christ! How did the disciples respond to this threat? Are there any lessons for us today? Let Scripture speak directly to us:

'On their release, Peter and John went back to their own people and reported all that the chief priests and elders had said to them. When they heard this, they raised their voices together in prayer to God. "Sovereign Lord," they said, "you made the heaven and the earth and the sea, and everything in them. You spoke by the Holy Spirit through the mouth of your servant, our father David:

'Why do the nations rage.
  and the peoples plot in vain?
The kings of the earth take their stand
  and the rulers gather together
against the Lord
  and against his Anointed One.'

Indeed Herod and Pontius Pilate met together with the Gentiles and the people of Israel in this city to conspire against your holy servant Jesus, whom you anointed. They did what your power and will had decided beforehand should happen. Now, Lord, consider their threats and enable your servants to speak your word with great boldness. Stretch out your hand to heal and perform miraculous signs and wonders through the name of your holy servant Jesus."

After they had prayed, the place where they were meeting was shaken. And they were all filled with the Holy Spirit and spoke the word of God boldly.'

(Acts 4:23–31, NIV, emphasis added)

When persecution and threat came it was met with prayer. The disciples of Jesus went to the other believers and prayed, not complained, or made plans of action, but prayed. Notice the content of their prayer. They prayed that God would increase the frequency and intensity of the miracles. They prayed for boldness to preach the Word of God. This is our great need for today, boldness to declare the Word of God.

Do you know how many pastors who have been intimidated so much by their church members or elders that they are unable to call a spade a spade? How many prophets have been silenced across this nation, and cannot preach the gospel without fear? Do you know how many ministers have been mesmerized, polarized and neutralized in the name of being politically correct? We need boldness back in our pulpits! Away with the kind of preaching that tries to please everyone and offend none!

Pastors, it is far better for you to be rejected by men but accepted and endorsed from where it matters most – heaven. What we all need at this hour is boldness! I prophesy that the spirit of Elijah is coming upon the Church. Pray for the spirit of boldness, the spirit that will be able to confront sin and compromise in high and low places, the spirit that will deliver the Word of the Lord without fear to those wielding political power, the spirit to go on TV and not water down the message of the gospel! O Lord, will you baptise us with this Pentecostal power we pray – Amen!

A lesson to all leaders (Acts 6:1–6)

As would be expected, when a church or organization begins to grow phenomenally, problems are bound to occur. The problem that confronted the early Church was that of neglecting the widows in the daily distribution of food. What were the apostles to do? Those of us in leadership positions often find ourselves overwhelmed by responsibilities. What is the right thing to do? How did the apostles respond in this instance? Simple, they looked at their God-given abilities and priorities and then found others to help them.

> 'So the Twelve gathered all the disciples together and said, "It would not be right for us to neglect the ministry of the word of God in order to wait on tables. Brothers, choose seven men from among you who are known to be full of the Spirit and wisdom. [In other words] we will turn this responsibility over to them and **will give our attention to prayer and the ministry of the word.**'

(Acts 6:2–4, NIV, emphasis added)

Notice what they said they would give their attention to – the ministry of the Word and prayer. As church leaders this is our primary assignment; if we fail here we fail in everything. Our lives must be given completely to prayer. There is barrenness in the ministry today because leaders have neglected the place of prayer. Sinners are flooding to hell today because we have neglected the prayer closet! Great Britain, indeed most of Europe, has become the Dark Continent today, because many of the shepherds are serving tables rather than fulfilling their function, prayer!

What was the outcome of their decision?

> 'So the word of God spread. The number of disciples in Jerusalem increased rapidly, and a large number of priests became obedient to the faith.'

(Acts 6:7, NIV)

Releasing Paul into the ministry (Acts 6:8–15; 7:1–60)

We have seen that as a result of the neglect of the widows in the daily food distribution, the apostles appointed the deacons. Stephen was the first and perhaps the most influential deacon.

Not only did God use him to do great wonders and miraculous signs, but he defended the faith with a wisdom that could not be withstood by his opponents. As is always the case throughout Church history, the enemies of Jesus set up a conspiracy against him. The consequence was that Stephen had to defend the faith. Inevitably he was up before the Sanhedrin accused of blasphemy. In reply Stephen launched into a long speech about Israel's relationship with God. Taking Israel's history he shared that the Jews had constantly rejected God's message and His prophets, and declared that the Sanhedrin had also rejected the Messiah, God's Son. What was the result of Stephen's speech?

> 'When they heard this, they were furious and gnashed their teeth at him. But Stephen, full of the Holy Spirit, looked up to heaven and saw the glory of God, and Jesus standing at the right hand of God. "Look," he said, "I see heaven open and Son of Man standing at the right hand of God."
>
> At this they covered their ears and, yelling at the top of their voices, they all rushed at him, dragged him out of the city and began to stone him. Meanwhile, the witnesses laid their clothes at the feet of a young man named Saul.
>
> While they were stoning him, Stephen prayed, "Lord Jesus, receive my spirit." Then he fell on his knees and cried out, "Lord, do not hold this sin against them." When he had said this, he fell asleep.'
>
> (Acts 7:54–60, NIV)

Just as his Lord had experienced, Stephen suffered from the hands of his opponents. Like his Master, instead of calling down a curse, he prayed for them: 'Lord, do not hold this sin against them.'

Interestingly we are told in Acts 8:1 that Paul was actually there, a witness giving approval to Stephen's death. I believe when Stephen was praying he was asking God not only to forgive his persecutors, but he was asking God to make his death count for His kingdom. I am convinced that it was the prayer of the first Christian martyr that produced the greatest apostle of all times, Paul. For it was shortly after that Saul, later Paul, was converted on the way to Damascus. As Church history has proved over the centuries, 'The blood of the martyrs is the seeds of the Church'.[27]

Prayer for the Holy Spirit (Acts 8:14–17)

We can further see the importance given to prayer in the early Church when Samaria accepted the gospel through the powerful ministry of Philip. They knew the importance of power from heaven above for service. What did they do?

> 'When the apostles in Jerusalem heard that Samaria had accepted the word of God, they sent Peter and John to them. When they arrived, they prayed for them that they might receive the Holy Spirit, because the Holy Spirit had not yet come upon any of them; they had simply been baptised into the name of the Lord Jesus. Then Peter and John placed their hands on them, and they received the Holy Spirit.'
>
> (Acts 8:14–17, NIV)

The dead raised Acts (9:36–43)

One of the greatest apologetics for our gospel is the raising of the dead. For our sin-loving, God-dishonouring, sceptical generation, nothing less will prove to them that Jesus is alive and is Lord over life and death! Not only did Jesus raise several dead Himself, but He charged His disciples to do the same, *'Heal the sick, raise the dead...'* (Matthew 10:8a, NIV).

In the book of Acts we are told that Peter, the chief spokesperson of the team, raised the dead.

'Peter went with them, and when he arrived he was taken upstairs to the room. All the widows stood around him, crying and showing him the robes and other clothing that Dorcas had made while she was still with them.

Peter sent them all out of the room; then he got down on his knees and prayed. Turning toward the dead woman, he said, "Tabitha, get up." She opened her eyes, and seeing Peter she sat up. He took her by the hand and helped her to her feet.'

(Acts 9:39–41, NIV)

Peter prayed and the dead woman was raised back to life. Prayer, faith-filled prayer, still raises the dead. What was the effect? There was massive publicity for the Church and many more were converted.

'This became known all over Joppa, and many people believed in the Lord.'

(Acts 9:42, NIV)

Gospel to the Gentiles (Acts 10:1–34)

Until now the good news of the kingdom had been restricted to Jews. Now God was ready to make people of every nationality partake of the gospel. It was a Roman centurion who had the privilege of hearing the gospel first. How did this happen? Oddly we are told that he prayed to God regularly even though he was a Gentile. We are told that because he gave alms to God and prayed regularly his faith was rewarded by a visit from an angel. Angels are not given the commission by God to preach the gospel, so God had to use a man to do it. It was a strange choice, the one who had so vehemently denied ever being associated with Jesus, Peter. We must remember how patriotic Peter was. The Word of the Lord that the good news was also meant for the Gentile world was given while Peter was praying.

> '*About noon the following day as they were on their journey and approaching the city, Peter went up on the roof to pray.*'
>
> (Acts 10:9, NIV)

Today we go on the roof to play, while the early Church went to pray. If we are ever going to have a vision for world mission, especially when we have so many prejudices, we must go to the place of prayer. Prayer will break our prejudices and make us see all human beings the way God sees them, potential sons of God, potential citizens of the kingdom of heaven.

Miracles happen when we pray (Acts 12:1–16)

One of the greatest and perhaps best examples of what happens when a church prays can be found in Acts chapter 12. Conversely, we can also see what can happen when we fall into a state of slumber. Lives, precious lives, can be lost! It seems to me that for once the early Church was asleep and needed waking up. 'What happened?' You might well ask. James, the leader of the Jerusalem church, was beheaded by Herod. I think it might perhaps have been because the Church was asleep. Obviously if you give the enemy a foothold, he will make it a stronghold. Because it pleased the Jews, Herod proceeded to arrest Peter also. I'm almost certain that he wanted to eliminate him just as he had done with James. This would have dealt a devastating blow to the early Church.

What was the Church to do? How would they respond? I'm sure someone would have challenged them to pray. After all, prayer is the greatest weapon the world has ever known. To their knees they went. They were convinced of their Lord's promise that the gates of hell shall not prevail against the army of the Lord.

Prayer changes things, particularly fervent prayer. We are told that the '*effectual fervent prayer of a righteous man avails much*'. We can see the early Church was a good match for the devil. While

Peter was locked in prison, with the intention of bringing him out for public trial and likely execution, the Church prayed.

> *'So Peter was kept in prison, but the church was earnestly praying to God for him.'*
>
> (Acts 12:5, NIV)

> *'... but long and fervent prayer was offered.'*
>
> (Weymouth)

> *'... but earnest prayer to God for him was persistently made by the Church.'*
>
> (Wms)

> *'... but there was a continued stream of prayer going up to God from the church on his behalf.'*
>
> (Knox)

What was the outcome? Miraculous escape! Today in Britain the Church is being attacked on all fronts by the enemy. Church leaders are being taken out by hell. The only language that the devil understands is force. This is what must return to the Church in Britain, persistent, agonizing, heartfelt prayer, prayer that will not take no for an answer, prayer that does not stop until we get the answer. This was the kind of prayer that released Peter! This kind of prayer is what will release many captives in this nation. Church, it's time to awake to battle! I am reminded of the old hymn:

> 'Onward, Christian soldiers, marching as to war,
> With the cross of Jesus going on before.
> Christ, the royal Master, leads against the foe;
> Forward into battle see His banners go!
>
> *Onward, Christian soldiers, marching as to war,*
> *With the cross of Jesus going on before.*

At the name of Jesus Satan's host doth flee;
On then, Christian soldiers, on to victory!
Hell's foundations quiver at the shout of praise;
Brothers, lift your voices, loud your anthems raise.

What the saints established that I hold for true ...

Onward then, ye people, join our happy throng,
Blend with ours your voices in the triumph song.
Glory, laud and honour unto Christ the King,
This through countless ages men and angels sing.

(Sabine Baring-Gould)

The Church and missionary enterprise (Acts 13:1–3)

Before Jesus ascended into heaven, He told His disciples that they would be endued with power from on high, after which they were to be a witness to the gospel first in Jerusalem, Judea, Samaria and unto the ends of the earth (Acts 1:8). As Christians, our responsibility is to take the good news to the ends of the world. However, the greatest obstacle to the fulfilment of the great commission is lack of personnel. Too many people are too comfortable in the Church today having a 'Holy Ghost Service' when the whole world around them is perishing. How did the early Church conquer this problem of apathy? They worshipped and fasted. I believe worship is the most powerful form of prayer. It does not just glorify God, it makes our hearts tender and sensitive to the Holy Spirit. This is one thing that we have lost in the Church today, which we must recover, a time or season of true worship, intimate worship with the Father. Remember the purpose for our existence, to worship the Father. The Father's eyes are running to and fro all over the earth to see those who will worship Him in Spirit and in truth. They also fasted, not feasted.

There's a time to feast and there should also be a time to fast. Many churches in the UK have lost the discipline of fasting. Too many pastors and church leaders have been given over to food. May God deliver us in the West from gluttony. The early Church worshipped and fasted.

> *'In the church at Antioch there were prophets and teachers: Barnabas, Simeon called Niger, Lucius of Cyrene, Manaen (who had been brought up with Herod the tetrarch) and Saul. While they were worshipping the Lord and fasting, the Holy Spirit said, "Set apart for me Barnabas and Saul for the work to which I have called them." So after they had fasted and prayed, they placed their hands on them and sent them off.'*
>
> (Acts 13:1–3, NIV)

When we spend time in worship, the Holy Spirit speaks. We will be more open to His direction. This was what happened in the early Church. The Holy Spirit spoke to set apart the duo of Barnabas and Saul for a missionary work. This is what we need in our fellowships today. Pastors and church leaders, let's spend quality time in the presence of the Father, worshipping Him and giving Him all the glory due His name! It is only in this kind of atmosphere that we can receive clear and definite instructions from Him.

The first missionary movement in the early Church was birthed out of prayer. How could we think we could carry out this important assignment without prayer? God help us. Send us on our knees! Give us the grace to spend quality time in Your presence.

Leadership and prayer (Acts 14:23)

Few would argue the critical place that spiritual leaders hold in God's kingdom. The wrong choice of a leader can dent the image of the Church and can do a lot of damage to the cause of Christ. Leaders need to be appointed carefully after serious prayer. Jesus prayed all night long before He chose His closest associates. Even then one of them still betrayed Him and many of them still demonstrated carnal behaviour. Not only do we need to appoint leaders in an atmosphere of prayer, we also need to pray for them continually, committing their assignments into the hands of God. This was one of the reasons why the early Church was strong, dynamic and had cutting edge leaders. What did Paul and Barnabas do?

> *'Paul and Barnabas appointed elders for them in each church and, with prayer and fasting, committed them to the Lord, in whom they had put their trust.'*
>
> (Acts 14:23, NIV)

It seems we cannot get past the issue of prayer and fasting. This was what the early Church leaders did, they prayed and fasted. This is what we need today. We must rediscover the importance of the discipline of fasting. Jesus prayed and fasted. Paul said, 'I fasted often.' Not sometimes, but often. The early Church fasted a great deal. The hypocrites fasted twice every week. The Church fathers fasted. John Wesley fasted. Hindus fast. Muslims fast. So, Church, why can we not fast? Let's awake to the discipline of fasting and we will begin to reap tremendous benefits.

The Church in Europe started in a prayer meeting (Acts 16:13–15)

Many people may be unaware that the first convert to Christianity in Europe was at a prayer meeting at Philippi. This should be an inspiration and a challenge to those of us living in Europe. Europe is the new Dark Continent.

'On the Sabbath we went outside the city gate to the river, where we expected to find a place of prayer. We sat down and began to speak to the women who had gathered there. One of those listening was a woman named Lydia, a dealer in purple cloth from the city of Thyatira, who was a worshipper of God. The Lord opened her heart to respond to Paul's message. When she and the members of her household were baptised, she invited us to her home, "If you consider me a believer in the Lord," she said, "come and stay at my house." And she persuaded us.'

(Acts 16:13–15, NIV)

Europe, God is calling us once again to provide places of prayer, houses of prayer. I can see twenty-four hours of prayer rising all across Great Britain. I see houses of prayer rising in Germany. I see the whole of Sweden engulfed in prayer. Norway, get ready because the fire of revival is coming. This is the season for prayer. Great Britain, awake to prayer! Remember when God wants to bless a nation or people, He will first of all set them praying. Europe, this is your hour of prayer and intercession! Enough of sleeping! Enough of slumbering! Enough playing church. It's the season to pray. It's the season to experience God's mercy. It's the season for revival!

Prison doors open (Acts 16:22–39)

A study of the history of the early Church will reveal that they suffered some severe persecution that seems odd to modern Christians. They were not only beaten but also thrown into prison for doing good deeds as we can read in Acts 16. Paul cast out the spirit of divination from a slave girl and the consequence was that they were stripped, beaten and placed in stocks in the inner cell. Despite this dismal situation, Paul and Silas praised God, praying and singing hymns to the Lord. They were simply fulfilling the Scripture 'in all things give thanks'.

*'About midnight Paul and Silas were praying and singing hymns
to God, and the other prisoners were listening to them. Suddenly
there was such a violent earthquake that the foundations of the
prison were shaken. At once all the prison doors flew open, and
everybody's chains came loose.'*

(Acts 16:25–26, NIV)

I see great persecution coming against the Church in Europe; it
will be almost unprecedented. Let the Church get ready. Let the
Church not count it strange when we begin to suffer persecution.
Great glory will come out of this persecution. The Church will
experience the supernatural workings of God like we have not
seen for many generations. We must handle persecution the way
Paul and Silas did. They did not complain. They didn't blame
God. They prayed and sang hymns to God. That's the way to
see God move on our behalf.

I also see a revival of the old hymns in the coming days. Many
of the hymns, composed over the centuries by revivalists and
reformers, will be sung again. Some will be sung with new tunes.
I see God using those old hymns powerfully in the coming days. I
see people weeping when these songs are sung. I see an army of
missionaries being raised again from this land. I see young men
and women, being raised by God, who will march across Europe.
They will go overseas to the Caribbean, into Asia and many of
them will go to Muslim nations. The hymns of Isaac Watts will be
of great inspiration to many.

Jesus shall reign where'er the sun
Does his successive journeys run;
His kingdom stretch from shore to shore,
Till moons shall wax and wane no more.

To Him shall endless prayer be made,
And praises throng to crown His head;

His Name like sweet perfume shall rise
With every morning sacrifice.

Suggested practical action

▶ Read through the book of Acts noting the place the early Church gave to prayer and the results of specific prayers.

▶ Read one book on soul winning a month.

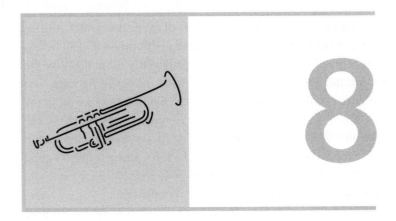

A Case for Christian Schools

*'All your children shall be taught by the L*ORD*,*
And great shall be the peace of your children.'
(Isaiah 54:13, NKJV)

'And these words which I command you today shall be in your heart.
You shall teach them diligently to your children, and shall talk of them
when you sit in your house, when you walk by the way, when you lie
down and when you rise up.'
(Deuteronomy 6:6–7, NKJV)

'For the sake of the Church, we must have and maintain Christian schools,' said Martin Luther. 'Christian education is not an option, it is an order: it is not a luxury, it is part of life. It is not something nice to have. It is not a part of the work of the Church; it is the work of the Church. It is not extraneous, it is essential. It is our obligation, not merely an option.'[28] This chapter is specifically directed at Christian leaders, leaders of denominations, Christian businessmen and women, Christians in education and all believers across this nation and beyond, particularly those that love the Lord and those that place great value on God's heritage, our children. This is a wake up call to the Church to wake-up to the reality of what is happening in our educational system. It is a call for all believers to help stem the tide of the massive destruction afflicted on our next generation. A nation's future is only as good as its children. If our children are morally and spiritually bankrupt, then there's no hope for our future as a nation.

Perhaps it might be helpful to tell my own story. I was raised in Nigeria, a member of the Commonwealth, with five other siblings. My parents are committed Christians, praise God! I was raised in a Christian environment. Going to church weekly was never optional. It was a duty we all had to perform. Perhaps one of the greatest legacies my parents gave me was sending me to their church school, a missionary school established by missionaries from Great Britain. As a young boy in a Baptist school, I was taught moral instruction, the basic values of honesty, integrity, compassion, love and humility. We were also taught honour and respect for all, particularly those in authority – church leaders, teachers and our parents. It was unheard of for a student to answer back, let alone disobey one's teacher. Every morning we attended morning assembly, and we were taught from God's holy book, the Bible.

Even when I went to secondary school to do my ordinary level and advanced level exams, things were virtually the same. The Bible was the centre of our education. There was no controversy about who created the world and everything in it. As I look back today, I often tell people that the greatest legacy I have after Christ Jesus was the Christian education my parents gave me. For this I am sincerely grateful. It is this legacy that I want to pass on to my biological and my spiritual children, to as many as the Lord wills.

For centuries, up to a couple of decades ago, Britain had the best education system in the world. It was the envy of other nations, developing and industrial. Most of the countries in Africa, Asia and South America model their education system on the British. Oxford and Cambridge Universities, the pride of our nation, are renowned throughout the world. Our children are taught to read and write to add and subtract and understand basic scientific principles. Text books in Britain taught the basics from a Christian ethical viewpoint. The Bible was read out loud at school every day, and scriptures were memorized. We were taught to pray together, to know the Ten Commandments, which in those days established moral absolutes.

We took the biblical injunction from the wise man Solomon to 'train up a child in the way he should go: and when he is old, he will not depart from it' (Proverbs 22:6, KJV) seriously both at school and at home. Discipline was not a problem. Teachers had the authority to discipline students whenever they went astray without any fear of being reprimanded by the authorities for child abuse. Neither were they afraid that the students would retaliate by attacking them physically.

Unfortunately things have gone rapidly downhill since the 1960s. Today the British educational system can truly be described as being in crisis. What went wrong?

There is an easy answer. Whereas before our textbooks were based upon and taught Christian values and principles, they have been replaced by textbooks based upon humanistic and New Age world-views. A short look at the textbooks and materials children use today will clearly show this. Not only has God been removed from first place in our textbooks and lesson outlines, the concept of moral absolutes has become a thing of the past. The Bible says,

> 'The way of a fool is right in his own eyes,
> But he who heeds counsel is wise.'

(Proverbs 12:15, NKJV)

As in the days of Judges, now everyone does what is *right in their own eyes*.

There has been an increase of serious problems in our schools for the last few decades, drug abuse, rape, abortions, gang warfare and sexually transmitted diseases. We now have the highest teenage pregnancy rate in Europe and the highest incidence of sexually transmitted diseases. The school system is in a moral freefall. Even Church schools funded by state support are often suffering the same moral decline.

I have seen that the educational system that was based on Christian principles and values worked well. Muslim leaders are as concerned as many Christians at the lack of moral guidance that is often the case in schools and are petitioning for Muslim schools in Britain to halt this decline. Meanwhile it is becoming increasingly difficult for Christian teachers to teach their pupils the basis for their own stance. However, the current system of education that our politicians are giving us based on secular humanist philosophy, which I prefer to call foreign, is failing our children woefully. Today we are reaping the fruit of five decades of neglect.

The conclusion is crystal clear. Let's go back to what worked. Let's go back to our foundation, which the present crop of politicians is trying to destroy. Let's go back to the system of education that brought honour, fame and greatness to our nation. Let's go back to the system of education that made us value and honour those in authority – parents, teachers and leaders. In the words of former Prime Minister John Major, 'Let's get back to basics.'

Unfortunately this possibility is not even considered by leaders. It seems to me that there are a few people in our government and educational authorities who have their own ungodly agenda. They are anti-Christian. They detest anything and everything that is linked to Christ. They would rather promote any other religion or ideology in our schools, as long as it is not Christian. Their agenda is to completely remove God, the Bible and

Christian prayer from our school system. They are anti-Christian in doctrine and disposition. They are the ones who would corrupt our children. They are bent on a route that will result in destroying your children and my children. This is why I have said in many places, including the Houses of Parliament, that I will do anything to fight against those who are bent on destroying those that God has put under my care, especially my own children. I will use all available resources to expose the folly of the ungodly and unprincipled few. Let me declare in prophecy to these folk. Your folly has been made manifest and you shall proceed and progress no further. Your humanistic agenda will no longer prosper in this nation in Jesus name.

The time has come for us in Britain to go back to our educational foundations, the educational system that we adopted for many centuries, which brought greatness, prosperity and progress to our nation. Let's go back to the foundation that our godly parents handed down to us:

> *'If the foundations are destroyed,*
> *What can the righteous do?'*
>
> (Psalm 11:3, NKJV)

Our ancestors who were Christians understood the biblical injunction in Deuteronomy chapter 6:

> *'And these words, which I command thee this day, shall be in thine heart: And thou shalt teach them diligently unto thy children.'*
> (Deuteronomy 6:6–7, KJV)

Our forefathers took the mandate to teach their children from the Word of God very seriously. Those parents taught their children stories from the Bible. The same took place in our schools. Every child knew how to memorize Scripture. From a very early age they knew the Lord's Prayer. They learned the Ten

Commandments by heart, which helped shape their relationship with God and man. However, things have changed today. Our children are taught primarily from a humanist agenda. This is why I shudder to leave my children in a state school. It is too dangerous to leave my precious children in the hands of those who teach that God does not exist, that He is simply a figment of our imagination. I am loath to leave my children, or any child for that matter, in the hands of those who don't believe in moral absolutes.

Christians in authority, rise up to protect Christian education!

I am pleading with pastors, church leaders, elders, deacons, denominations and businessmen and women across the British Isles to rise up in support of Christian education. Businessmen and women, with financial resources, I believe, it is no coincidence that you are reading this book now. I believe God has raised you up into the kingdom for such a time as this. I believe there is burden in the heart of God for the Church to catch the vision for Christian education. There's a cry in the Spirit for the Church in Britain to invest in Christian education. Our schools and indeed our children are the targets of the enemy.

One day I discovered via the ministry of John Mulinde, a man greatly used by God in the current revival in Uganda, the precepts of the New Age put forward by Alice Bailey. Alice Bailey had a ten-point strategy to change Europe to a humanist and atheistic society. One of her key strategies was to let parents alone, but target their children. According to her, if you get the children you will get a whole nation. How true this is! A look at Britain today will reveal that Alice Bailey's strategies have worked. There's a whole generation, I call them the spoilt generation, who are without knowledge of the Lord or His works. Humanists and New Agers have targeted our schools and they seem to be succeeding. This trend will continue unless the Church wakes up and does something about this. Recently a Christian sister gave me a book that I'm sure will shock you as much as it did me. According to the Humanist Manifesto I and II:

- 'Humanists regard the universe as self-existing and not created.
- The human species is an emergence from natural evolutionary forces.
- We reject all religions, ideological or moral codes that suppress freedom (or) dull intellect.
- The right to birth control, abortion and divorce should be recognized.
- Individuals should be permitted to express their sexual ... lifestyles as they desire.
- Promises of immortal salvation or fear of eternal damnation are both illusory and harmful. There is no credible evidence that life survives the death of the body.' [29]

The *Humanist Magazine*, January/February, 1983, says:

'The battle for mankind's future must be waged and won in the public school classroom by teachers who correctly perceive their role as they proselytize a new faith; a religion of humanity ... Utilizing a classroom instead of a pulpit to convey humanist values in whatever subject they teach. The classroom must and will become an arena of conflict between the old and the new – the rotting corpse of Christianity, together with all its adjacent evils and misery and the new faith of humanism.' [30]

It is clear to me the agenda has been set. The strategies are in place. The battle line has been drawn. In view of this information what are you going to do? How are you acting as a church leader, prayer warrior, pastor or a businessman? What about you, Christian parent? Are we all going to pretend that we don't know what is at stake? Will my sword rest when the enemy is at the gate? Should I keep quiet when the destiny of a whole generation is at stake? Will I say nothing so as not to lose my reputation, indeed if I ever had one? Am I going to do as my predecessors have done? My sword cannot rest. The Holy Spirit of God within me will not permit me. I cannot ignore the call of destiny. The stakes are too high. The calling is too grand. It's time to speak up or forever remain silent. Our children will never forgive us when they find out we had the knowledge and the ability to do something but did nothing. The challenge of Mordecai to Esther confronts me,

> *'For if you remain completely silent at this time, relief and deliverance will arise for the Jews from another place ... Yet who knows whether you have come to the kingdom for such a time as this?'*
>
> (Esther 4:14, NKJV)

This is the time for the Church to rise up to the importance of Christian education, and by this I mean Christ-centred education. This is the time for all denominations, Christian ministries and churches to consider setting up our own schools if we are not already doing so. It doesn't matter how insignificant it may look today, remember we should never despise the day of 'small beginnings'.

Britain's sex education needs changing

I am committing my views on sex education in Britain in print for two major reasons. First, to decline do so would be doing a huge disservice to this nation. It was Leonard Ravenhill who remarked, 'Let none fail to realize that to keep silent while a house is burning is criminal. He is not a comforter who lets his neighbor sleep as he watches a criminal move to the door with a gun.'[31]

Secondly, because I believe many people, including some parents, are ignorant about what is actually taught in sex education in our schools. Most pastors who have a responsibility to inform and educate their congregations are themselves ignorant, some out of choice. Everywhere I have shared this information, without exception, I have seen parents and pastors alike groan and grind their teeth in utter disbelief. I want you to get ready to be shocked. It is not for the faint-hearted. My belief is that what is taught as sex education in Britain is nothing but pornography and an encouragement to introduce sexual activities to our children as early as possible. I believe that it is not appropriate to expose children to sexual information too early. It destroys their childhood and can cause lifelong emotional pain. We should resist the humanist hidden agenda behind sex education.

Pastors, we need to give our congregations clear guidance over sexual issues because of the health risks involved in some sexual behaviour including AIDS. In Africa we have a good example of the kind of advice I am advocating. Uganda has reduced the incidence of AIDS from 30% to 10% by its strong educational programme, in conjunction with the churches, especially the Anglican Church. It's as easy as A B C: A, abstain; B, be faithful in marriage; and only if you refuse to do either, then C, use a condom. Only in the north of the country is AIDS still on the increase, where they are still experiencing a regime of institutionalized child abuse that has gone on for the last eighteen years. Pastors, how would you advise the mother having to answer her eight-year-old son the answer to 'Mummy, where are the condoms?' in the supermarket? Some companies have a vested financial interest in sex education at the earliest possible age because they will profit by increased sales of contraceptives. Our children are their potential market and as such they are a major target.

Sex education encourages gay sex

This may sound as if I am trying to exaggerate but, believe it or not, our children are being told to try sex with children of the same sex. In an article in the *Sunday Times* of 30 January 2000, the reports had the caption 'Schools video tells children to try gay sex'. The story reads: 'A video that encourages school children as young as 14 to experiment with gay sex has caused outrage among MPs and family campaigners. The film, according to the reports, "now available in 180 schools" also asked pupils aged 14–16 to discuss whether a fictional 15 year old boy, Michael, should have unprotected gay sex with his boyfriend.'

In the same video a young college student called Karl tells his audience of school pupils that to obtain sexual satisfaction they should '**try experimenting with boys and girls to see whom they feel most comfortable with**'. The video also shows young people talking about 'Coming out' and their experience of homosexual relationships and includes **images of young gay couples kissing**. It is absolutely clear to me that there is a hidden agenda by some ungodly few to encourage our children into gay relationships. I wonder how many parents would want their children exposed to this kind of video. I wonder how many pastors, elders and church leaders have seen this article? If we have, what have we done or what are we doing? Sometimes we can be too heavenly minded to be of any earthly use!

Sex education for eleven year olds

If the story above didn't shock you maybe this one will. When I read this story I realized how debased our society has become. I began to realize how serious the battle we are fighting in our educational system is. I became even more alarmed, when I discovered what was recommended in the borough where I live.

A Christian information leaflet had the following information (referring to a video and resource material produced by Avon Health Promotion Services for school governors and teachers responsible for how sex education is taught in a school context) under the heading '**Condomania: using the male and female condom**'.

The instruction reads:

> 'After demonstrating the proper use of condom, encourage the young people to have a go themselves at an appropriate time. This can include practising by putting a condom on the next time they masturbate. You can suggest to them that this is very useful practice for the first time they will use one **with a partner.**' [32]

The same sex education material for children over age eleven continues:

> 'Discuss the issue of buying condoms over the counter at a chemist. Focus on how young people can be embarrassed and how they can overcome this. Develop this work into small role-plays where young people practise the words they would use to buy condoms in a chemist. **A useful home-work task is for young people to actually go into a chemist and buy condoms** and report back on what it was like, how they felt, how they could make it easier next time etc.'

Did you really read that? Eleven-year-old children were to be taught how to put on condoms. It says the teachers should suggest to the children that it is a very useful practice for the first time they will use one with a partner. To teach eleven-year-old children how to use a condom is to destroy their innocence too early.

Furthermore, according to these unprincipled and ungodly educators, a homework task for these young children was for them to actually go into a chemist to buy condoms and report back. Who would take them to the chemist? They are still too young to be out on their own. It's against the law until they are fourteen. Besides, the time would be better spent concentrating on their English, mathematics, science and other assignments. Our educators, backed up by our government, paid for by our taxes think the best assignment for an eleven-year-old boy or girl is to go and buy a condom. Shame on our government! Shame on those who came up with this idea! If I had not seen the leaflet myself, I would never have thought that this would be possible in a nation whose foundation was built on Christian principles. I began to write this chapter in Nairobi, Kenya in the home of a godly Christian couple. They were so taken aback that they were speechless. They could not believe that Britain had stooped to this level. This couple had been planning to send their son to Britain for his secondary education. Needless to say, after reading the sex education pamphlet, they cancelled the idea.

I don't know whether pastors and church leaders are taking this to heart. In view of this information, how are we going to equip our members to overcome this satanic agenda? What are we going to do to stem this tide? It seems to me that while we slept, the enemy came in and he has dealt an almost fatal blow to our educational system. It's high time we pastors joined the public debate. We should also take care to provide opportunity for the fundamental biblical teaching to be given to our members and give these issues a regular place in our intercession.

Generally speaking the message that is going out across Great Britain today is that of the practice of 'safe-sex'. This is being widely propagated through literature distributed by family planning clinics, health centres, youth clubs, drop-in centres, promotion units and schools.

So what is the message of sex-education?

First, sex education adopts an amoral position. In other words having sex in whatever form is not a moral issue. There's no moral framework to guide our children when it comes to the issue of sex. Obviously this comes out of the humanist agenda. As far as sex is concerned, according to the preaching of our sex educators, nothing is right or wrong. We only do what we believe to be right. Therefore it is perfectly okay for two children as young as twelve to have sex together. Also for two teenage boys to have gay sex is perfectly in order! This was exactly the situation in Israel in one of the darkest periods of its history – the time of Judges. Again and again the book of Judges repeats the refrain, *'In those days there was no king in Israel; everyone did what was right in his own eyes'* (e.g. Judges 21:25, NKJV).

Because our young children are told that they can do whatever seems right to them, there's therefore nothing wrong with having sex with as many partners as possible, what we used to call promiscuous sex. Also, because nothing is wrong in itself, homosexual relationships are perfectly in order!

The truth is our sexual conduct raises fundamental dilemmas, which we cannot just pretend do not exist. This is what our young ones face every day with our sex education programme. For example, is it wrong to have an abortion? Is it right to cheat on one's partner? Is it right to have homosexual relationships? Is it right to have sex before marriage? These are important questions, which everyone, particularly the young ones, must answer!

Let's take a look at some of the pamphlets used to promote sex education. The pamphlet, *Sexual Health Matters for Young Women* states:

'whether or not you have sex can be a difficult decision to make. But in the end it's what's right for you, and only you can answer that. If you decided you're not ready for sex then fine.'

It continues: 'you should "only have sex because you want to".' [33]

Sex is for pleasure

The second important message being propagated by our sex education programme is that sex is for your personal pleasure. This is contrary to what the Bible teaches, that sex is meant to be enjoyed to celebrate one's love in the committed covenant relationship of marriage. Our sex education programme actually sees marriage as an obstacle, because it restricts sexual freedom! The premise upon which this lie is built is that all children want to enjoy sexual pleasure once they reach puberty and they should not be denied this pleasure. Could this also be the reason why many parents today are not so concerned about whether or not their children have sex? What's important is that they are protected from sexually transmitted diseases and unwanted pregnancies!

Our sex education programme teaches that the primary purpose of sex is to receive and give pleasure! A pamphlet from Brook Advisory Centres explains that 'it takes time to learn how to be a good lover'. You need to know your own body first and what pleases you, find out how many ways you can give yourself pleasure. You need to know your partner and what pleases him or her. You need to feel at ease with each other. What turns you on? What turns your partner on? Can you talk about it? Remember – it does not have to be a sexual intercourse. So don't rush. Feel safe and be safe. Learn to share with your partner how many ways you can give and receive pleasure.[34]

The question is why Great Britain has the highest rate of teenage pregnancies in Western Europe. Why should sexually transmitted diseases not reach alarming or epidemic proportions in this nation as our national papers have reported lately? Why would abortion figures not continue to soar among our young people? The truth is things will continue to go downhill because the enemy has been propagating a lie, which has been bought by our nation! Why won't things get worse when the Church, which is supposed to be the light, is filled with darkness? Why shouldn't things get even worse because the Church is fast asleep? How should the Church be responding? I believe we should not be afraid to instruct our young people about sex. We should teach sex education from the biblical perspective.

Abstinence outside marriage

I will repeat, as I have said elsewhere in many places, what we should be teaching our children and youth is abstinence until married. This is what the Bible teaches, and this is what is taught in many places. The Bible not only teaches us to flee sexual immorality, but it encourages us to say no to ungodly passions:

> *'Flee also youthful lusts; but follow righteousness, faith, charity, peace, with them that call on the Lord out of a pure heart.'*
>
> (2 Timothy 2:22, KJV)

> *'. . . encourage the young men to be self-controlled.'*
>
> (Titus 2:6, NIV)

> *'For the grace of God . . . teaches us to say "No" to ungodliness and worldly passions, and to live self-controlled, upright and godly lives in this present age.'*
>
> (Titus 2:11–12, NIV)

I wonder why, in spite of all ample evidence from America where abstinence education has been taught and sexually transmitted diseases and abortion among young people have been drastically lowered, our government is not following suit? These are the kind of issues with which I believe the Church should be confronting our government! This is the only way to bring about reformation in our society. Rather than isolate ourselves, God wants us to engage and be involved in government.

Suggested practical action

▶ I encourage you to research the humanist agenda typified by Alice Bailey to change Europe to a humanistic and atheistic society.

▶ I encourage all parents to visit their children's school and request a copy of their sex education curriculum. I believe you have the right to protest if there is anything pornographic or indecent.

▶ I encourage churches, ministries and Christian leaders to work more closely, so that our voices can be heard when we speak with one voice.

▶ I encourage parents and church leaders not to shy away from teaching on the subject of sex education. I believe we need to develop a wholesome public alternative.

▶ Write to your MP about promoting sexual abstinence outside marriage in the interest of building a stable society, encouraging traditional families and promoting traditional family values via the taxation system.

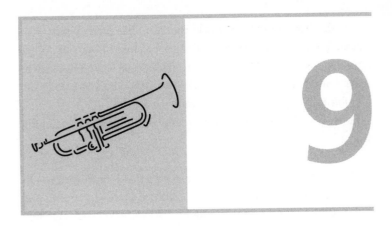

What Happened to the Great Commission?

'He who gathers crops in summer is a wise son,
  but he who sleeps during harvest is a disgraceful son.'
(Proverbs 10:5, NIV)

Before Jesus ascended into heaven, He gave the Church a command to make Him known throughout the whole world. This is what is referred to as the Great Commission. It is the Great Commission because it is a divine assignment and because we are to tell the greatest story ever told – the story of God's love for humanity.

Such is the love that He gave up His only son to die for the world.

> 'For God so loved the world that he gave his one and only Son, that whoever believes in him shall not perish but have eternal life.'
> (John 3:16, NIV)

It is the story to tell the world that God has made peace with mankind and that He's no longer angry because of our sins! What a privilege we have. This was what made Jesus leave His glory in heaven and become a man, suffering on Golgotha's tree. He said, *'It is finished!'* The way to God is now clear!

However, shortly before He ascended, He gave us marching orders:

> *'Therefore go and make disciples of all nations, baptising them in the name of the Father and of the Son and of the Holy Spirit, and teaching them to obey everything I have commanded you. And surely I am with you always, to the very end of the age.'*
>
> (Matthew 28:19–20)

Since these marching orders over two thousand years ago, Christ has not revoked them. In this chapter I challenge the Church in Britain to rise up to the all-important assignment of soul-winning. There are at least four other commands to go and win souls in the New Testament: Mark 16:15, Luke 24:46–48, John 20:21 and Acts 1:8.

In Mark 16:15–16 we read,

> *'Go into all the world and preach the good news to all creation. Whoever believes and is baptised will be saved, but whoever does not believe will be condemned.'*
>
> (NIV)

In Luke 24:46–48 we read,

> *'He told them, "This is what is written: The Christ will suffer and rise from the dead on the third day, and repentance and forgiveness of sins will be preached in his name to all nations, beginning at Jerusalem. You are witnesses . . . "'*
>
> (NIV)

In John 20:21 Jesus further clarified what our vocation should be, sent out ones, missionaries (the term 'missionary' actually means 'someone sent out with a message'):

> *'Again Jesus said, "Peace be with you! As the Father has sent me, I am sending you."'*
>
> (NIV)

Finally, in Acts 1:8, Jesus not only gives us what our vocation should be, but also sets out the scope of our assignment, to the ends of the earth:

> *'But you will receive power when the Holy Spirit comes on you; and you will be my witnesses in Jerusalem, and in all Judea and Samaria, and to the ends of the earth.'*
>
> (NIV)

Priority number one

When I was in secondary school I took economics as a subject. One of the things we studied is called the 'scale of preference'. The scale of preference is a way of organizing things to do, depending on their importance. First on the list goes the most important, the most pressing need, the task that absolutely has to be done. Further down goes everything else, based on how important they are to us. Each of us will have a different list. The same system applies to the Church. We are supposed to have a scale of preference, with our most important assignments topping the list. From my understanding of Scripture, I believe the most important assignment of the Church, of any church, is winning souls into the kingdom. This should be our number one priority. This should always be number one on our agenda, number one in our prayers, number one in our budget, number one during eldership meetings, and number one to every believer!

Therefore any church that does not put soul winning as its number one priority is only majoring in the minor.

Outside Christ is outside in everything

The picture that the Bible paints of people outside of Christ is very gloomy. Man is simply lost and hopeless. By man I mean the whole spectrum of humanity. Hebrew, like French, uses the masculine plural for any group of people, young and old, good and bad, rich or poor, well-educated or simple minded. It's just a plural noun. Any group of people that includes male and female is included in the Hebrew. Only if the whole group is female is the feminine plural form used. I mean no disrespect; I just use the term 'man' as a convenient plural noun.

To recap, man is lost outside Christ, lost, wandering aimlessly through life on the edge of a precipice. Man is lost not just because of the sins he has committed, but because he was born in sin. We are sinners in both senses, sinners because we have sinned, and we sin because to do the wrong thing is inherent in our nature. It does not matter the colour of our skin, race, language, ethnicity, education – outside of Christ we are lost!

> 'For all have sinned and fall short of the glory of God.'
>
> (Romans 3:23, NIV)

> 'All of us have become like one who is unclean,
>   and all our righteous acts are like filthy rags;
> we all shrivel up like a leaf,
>   and like the wind our sins sweep us away.'
>
> (Isaiah 64:6, NIV)

The Bible teaches that there is a penalty for sin. If something is wrong it is absolutely wrong, so if someone's action is a sin then they have done something wrong and punishment has been earned. Punishment for sin is death. Because of the original sin of Adam in the Garden of Eden all humanity has been sentenced to death. But, praise God, Jesus took our place and died in our place as a substitute sacrifice! He has therefore paid for our sin and hands His action's reward to us – life!

> *'For the wages of sin is death, but the gift of God is eternal life in Christ Jesus our Lord.'*
>
> (Romans 6:23, NIV)

If man outside of Christ is lost and will spend eternity in hell unless he accepts the free offer of Christ, then what greater assignment could the Church have than using all of our resources in getting the message out as fast as we can and as far as we can? This is what made the great in Great Britain. At one time she was the number one missionary sending nation. It was the love of God for lost humanity that created the missionary organizations and spent several thousands, if not millions of pounds, in this eternal mission. How well, one may ask, is the Church in the UK fulfilling the Great Commission now? I strongly believe that, as in most areas, we are asleep. Solomon says,

> *'He who gathers in summer is a wise son,*
> *He who sleeps in harvest is a son who causes shame.'*
>
> (Proverbs 10:5, NKJV)

A wise son, and I dare say a wise leader, and a wise church will gather crops in summer, but a disgraceful son or church sleeps during harvest! The question is, are we the wise or disgraceful son?

Around two million people in Britain would call themselves Christian. If this is true, why do we have so many all around us who are unbelievers? Why are we hearing reports by important Church leaders such as Cardinal O'Connor that this nation cannot be considered a Christian nation? Why would Britain, a once Christian nation, now be called a society of atheists by the former Archbishop of Canterbury? Surely it's because the Church has ceased to be outward looking.

We must always remember that the lost coin must be found, the lost sheep must be recovered, the prodigal son must come back home, we must go to the highways and the byways and compel them to come in. Like a careful farmer at lambing time we must always think of those who are outside the fold. It is our responsibility to rescue the perishing.

> 'Rescue the perishing, care for the dying
> Snatch them in pity from sin and the grave
> Weep over the erring one, care for the dying
> Tell them of Jesus the mighty to save
> Rescue the perishing, care for the dying
> Jesus is merciful, Jesus will save!'

(Fanny J. Crosby)

Another songwriter wrote:

> 'Why are we living a life, full of pleasures and simplicity?
> Why do we sing songs to God?
> When the whole world refuses to believe!
> No one is telling the world anymore that the Saviour is
>   going to return!
> Tell me, if you don't tell the sinner
> Tell me how will they know the Lord,
> Someone has got to tell the world that Jesus is on His way
> Someone has got to tell the world that they must be
>   born-again!' [35]

Many of the churches in the UK suffer from 'fellowship-itis'. This happens when fellowships go sour. From the Scriptures we are told that fellowship is a healthy thing for a believer and we should endeavour not to forsake the gathering of the saints. However, when believers continue to look inwards, they concentrate on meeting the needs of those in the fold rather than reach out to new souls. The Church then begins to suffer from 'fellowship-itis'. The Church is supposed to be a labour ward, where we give birth to new souls. That's what the fold is for, a safe place to give birth. Every member of a fellowship ought to be a soul winner, a midwife if you like. Pastors, it is our responsibility to lead the way in this most important area. It is our responsibility to present the vision, coordinate strategy and to lead by example! I know how difficult this can be. I'm a pastor. Many issues, projects and people will pull you in different directions but we must make up our minds as to what is our priority and put everything into it.

Other people can do it, so can we

I believe the Church has a lot to learn from the Mormons and the Jehovah's Witnesses. They are doing the job. Soul winning, or what we may call proselytising, is very critical to these two organizations. Mormons give two years of their lives into going to share the message of the 'good news'. I am always convicted and challenged whenever I have a Jehovah's Witness knock at my door. I often feel like covering my face in shame because I know that this is what I am supposed to be doing, yet spend so little time doing it! It is time to wake up! It is harvest time in God, so get out there before we lose them!

The harvest will not always be there. We are in the race of life. It is a matter of life and death.

We're the spiritual emergency service

All of us living in the UK and in the developed world understand well the importance of the emergency services. By this I mean the people who answer when 999 is called – the fire brigade, police and the ambulance service. Time is so crucial. There is a 'golden hour' to treat casualties. Resuscitate well within the first hour after injury and the patient has the best chance of recovery. Delay can lead to all manner of complications. A response service has to act swiftly. They must take notice of the time and get there fast, as failure to respond immediately to calls may result in lives being lost!

I believe the world values timing more when it comes to delivering their responsibility. Little wonder then that the Lord said:

> *'For the people of this world are more shrewd* [wiser] *in dealing with their own kind than are the people of the light.'*
>
> (Luke 16:8b, NIV)

Leonard Ravenhill wrote:

> 'Could a mariner sit idle if he heard the drowning cry?
> Could a doctor sit in comfort and just let his patients die?
> Could a fireman sit idle, let men burn and give no hand?
> Can you sit at ease in Zion with the world around you
>   damned?' [36]

Let's hear what the Lord has to say through the wise man Solomon about our assignment and the consequences of ignoring it:

> *'Rescue those being led away to death;*
> *   hold back those staggering toward slaughter.*
> *If you say, "But we knew nothing about this,"*
> *   does not he who weighs the heart perceive it?*
> *Does not he who guards your life know it?*
> *   Will he not repay each person according to*
> *   what he has done?'*
>
> (Proverbs 24:11–12, NIV)

Church, it is time to wake up to our responsibilities. It is time to obey your marching orders. It is time to arise from slumber and save the perishing. It is time to go to the street corners sharing the message of saving grace. It is time to snatch folk from the fire. It is time to invest your life in eternity. It is time to get to work to see Britain and indeed the whole of Europe saved. It is time to share the gospel.

Suggested practical action

▶ I encourage pastors and church leaders to do a review of all their ministry activities and see what place they give to soul winning.

▶ I encourage church leaders, if they are not already doing this, to have classes where they can teach and equip the saints on the all-important assignment of soul winning.

▶ Senior pastors should make proven ability to win souls one of their criteria when choosing those to help them on their ministry team and ensure that it continues to be actively practised by all on the leadership team.

▶ Churches should create ways of affirming and encouraging soul winners.

The Shaking is Coming

'This is what the LORD Almighty says: "In a little while I will once more shake the heavens and the earth, the sea and the dry land. I will shake all nations, and the desired of all nations will come, and I will fill this house with glory," says the LORD Almighty.'
(Haggai 2:6–7, NIV)

God has spoken clearly that in these last days the heavens will be shaken. The earth too will be shaken. The sea will be shaken. The dry land will be shaken! Every nation will be shaken! No nation will escape. Indeed it has already begun, tsunami, earthquake damage, mud slides, and bombs exploding in London, attacks on world finance centres, life savings wiped out by pension companies, families split apart by divorce, drugs or stress-related problems. The traditional supports are disappearing fast, casualties to changing attitudes, values and corruption. I believe a great shaking is coming to Great Britain.

Both in the Old Testament and the New the same warning is written. It is brought into focus in the New Testament when the writer of Hebrews declares:

> 'At that time his voice shook the earth, but now he has promised, "Once more I will shake not only the earth but also the heavens." The words "once more" indicate the removing of what can be shaken – that is, created things – so that what cannot be shaken may remain.'
>
> (Hebrews 12:26–27, NIV)

What will be shaken? Anything and everything that moves, in other words everything that can be shaken will be. Nothing will be exempt. Political institutions of centuries are going to be shaken. Get ready! We are going to see major changes in British politics. Parliament will be shaken, individual politicians, those 'movers and shakers' and the untouchables will be shaken!

I also believe a great shake-up is coming to the media. You can expect to see well-known, long-established media companies going to the wall. Already we see unprecedented numbers of people filing for bankruptcy. Those responsible for the films and programmes that corrupt the minds of our young ones will come under the judgment of God. Overnight they will come to judgment. No church will be spared. Be sure judgment will start in the Church. Alcoholics who beat their wives in secret, those who abuse their children will be exposed; those who preach a message of love then go home to strike their kids for any minor infringement of their petty rules will come under the judgment of Almighty God.

God is going to shake many leaders. Many who have lived a life of dishonesty and deceit will be exposed. Many churches that are not honouring Jesus, those who are not concerned about the state of the sheep, will be closed overnight.

May I say that the shaking that God is bringing upon the Body of Christ is to bring a separation between human effort and God-determined action. God will shake everything that is man-made. Everything that has been built on shaky foundations, everything that is not built on Christ, everything that will not stand the test of fire, will be brought down.

> *'That no flesh should glory in his presence.'*
>
> (1 Corinthians 1:29, KJV)

Only what is of eternal value will remain. I believe the pyramid structure of authority is going to experience God's shaking. Those who have ruled the Church of Christ as their own personal empire will suddenly disappear. The wind of change is coming upon the Church. There's a change coming in the way we 'do church'. Everything that has been exalting itself against the knowledge of God will be brought down under the judgment of God.

A word for those who lead the Church

In view of the approaching shaking, what manner of men should we be? What should we be doing? I say this with humility in my heart knowing how susceptible I am myself. It is time to do a clean-up exercise. It is time to do an appraisal, to take a long, hard look at our own practice, an overhaul of our ministry apparatus. Are there any projects or programmes that are not commanded by God? Is there anything done out of selfish ambition or motives? The apostle Paul in his letter to the Philippians warns,

> *'Do nothing out of selfish ambition or vain conceit.'*
>
> (Philippians 2:3, NIV)

It is time to repent of every work of the flesh. It is time to repent for taking advantage of the people of God. It is time we pastors repented of control and manipulation! It is time to repent of not equipping and releasing the saints into the ministry, rather than controlling them. It is time we repent of our prayerlessness, apathy and compromise! It is time we repent for not being able to speak up for truth. It is time we set our houses in order before the shaking comes. We should pray like David:

> *'Search me, O God, and know my heart;*
>   *try me and know my anxious thoughts.*
> *See if there is any offensive way in me,*
>   *and lead me in the way everlasting.'*
>
> (Psalm 139:23–24, NIV)

Suggested practical action

▶ Pray that God will show you anything that is displeasing to Him and repent.

▶ Pray that when the shaking occurs you will recognize God's hand behind the events and put your trust firmly in the Lord.

▶ Pray that God will help church leaders to review their activities and remove anything that is displeasing to Him.

▶ Prophesy that all man-made practices and programmes in the Church will stop.

Islam is Advancing in Britain

*'If you forsake the LORD, and serve foreign gods, then He will turn
and do you harm and consume you, after He has done you good ...
put away the foreign gods which are among you, and incline your
heart to the LORD God of Israel.'*
(Joshua 24:20, 23, NKJV)

Events of recent times include the attacks on the World Trade
Center, the Madrid bombings and the two bombings in London.
In reprisal invasions of Afghanistan and Iraq have taken place.
The establishment of peaceful democracy in Iraq that Saddam
Hussein was thought to be blocking is proving difficult to
establish, and emphasizes the threat to global security from
suicide terrorists. The use of suicide bombers is not new; towards
the end of the Second World War the Japanese were employing
similar tactics with their kamikaze pilots. However, what is
new is the deliberate targeting of civilians to create maximum

fear and to influence political decisions. Targets for this new terror tactic are highly symbolic, including humanitarian organization personnel, and are timed to create erosion of trust in democratic leaders.

Al Quaeda has been blamed by George W. Bush for much of the recent high profile events, but there has been little obvious result from the hunt for Osama Bin Laden, the leader of this new terror. What is obvious is that the terrorists have all been identified as Muslims.

We need to know the time spiritually and have a clear understanding of Christian values if we are to understand and pray strategically for our country. The latest information about who are directly responsible for the London bombings is that they are, or were, Muslims brought up in the UK, but disaffected with the status quo, who have come to believe they are serving the higher purpose of the will of Allah. This does not mean that there is universal support for global terror by the Muslim community at large, but does point us to the need to understand Islamic thought and the Qur'an passages which have been interpreted by some Muslim clerics as being supportive of these tactics to advance Islam.

Historically many countries in the Middle East and Central Asia, reaching as far east as the most westerly parts of China – which is now called Xinjang province or the Autonomous Uighur Region – were either Christian, of the Nestorian denomination (the church whose patriarch resides in Baghdad), or Buddhist. Armed conflicts along the 'Silk Road', a series of trading routes linking the Far East with Europe, brought Muslim traders into contact with indigenous people groups and by successive military action imposed Islam as the religion of the territory. The last massacre of Christians in the town of Kashgar wiped out a generation of believers who had become established just prior to the Second World War. Even today travellers to the region may be warned of the dangers, and Han Chinese who are encouraged by the Chinese government to settle there, are afraid of the fiery tempers and sharp knives carried by Muslim Uighurs.

Iran, Saudi Arabia, Iraq and the Gulf States, all have strict anti-alcohol laws, restrict the lives of women and run their societies as patriarchal communities where double standards can often be observed. Islam is a religion which declares it is every Muslim's duty to proselytise and to work for the establishing of Islamic territorial control. This concept is quite different from Christianity. The Bible declares *'The earth is the* LORD*'s'* (Exodus 9:29; Psalm 24:1, NKJV) and we are to steward God's world wisely and fairly.[37]

Our biblical mandate is to share that there is salvation in one name only, the name of Jesus who died, was resurrected and who ascended to heaven and who now resides in us by the Holy Spirit. Our motivation for proclaiming the good news is one of gratitude to God for allowing us to escape from the consequences of our own rebellion against Him, and sharing that message of hope and love with humanity. We may sometimes use the language of warfare but this war, it is clear, is one of prayer. Our battle with spiritual forces is in heavenly places, not the taking up of weapons to impose doctrine on reluctant victims such as happened in the Middle Ages. The weapons of our warfare are not earthly ones:

> *'For the weapons of our warfare are not carnal but mighty in God for pulling down strongholds, casting down arguments and every high thing exalts itself against the knowledge of God.'*
>
> (1 Corinthians 10:4–5a, NKJV)

Let us consider some of the Qur'an passages which indicate that the intention of Muslims is to disseminate their religion, with its accompanying legal structure Shariah law, throughout the world. The Rev. M.J. Fisher has been involved in a service ministry to Muslims for decades. He has posted a book entitled

A Topical Study of the Qur'an on the internet at www.answering-islam.org. I quote from the August 2005 update,

> 'Muslims fight everyone who rejects Islam, even Christians and Jews, until they pay regular financial tribute with willing submission and feel themselves to completely subjected to their Islamic conquerors (9:29).' [38]

The Muslim Manifesto states:

> 'Jihad is a basic requirement of Islam and living in Britain or having British nationality by birth or naturalization does not absolve the Muslim from his or her duty to participate in Jihad; this participation can be active service in armed struggle abroad and/or the provision of material and moral support to those engaged in such struggle anywhere in the world.' [39]

Extreme sects of Islam often use the term *Jihad* in a literal, military sense. However this is not the only interpretation of this word. The word *Jihad* means 'struggle'. It is often translated 'holy war', but the majority of Muslims understand this to be an active mental process to bring their actions into surrender to the one God, Allah.[40]

The duty to create an Islamic state wherever Muslims live has even led to attempts to convert the Royal Family. One letter distributed at a rally for Islam III on Wednesday 22 July 1998 held in Trafalgar Square, London organized in conjunction with Al-Muhajiroun, exhorted Queen Elizabeth to become a Muslim:

> '... Embrace Islam and reject the evil ideologies man has made, like Monarchies, capitalism and communism and their evil concepts such as secularism, liberalism, nationalism, patriotism and the rule of the people i.e. democracy which

have led to the destruction of man's life, honour, dignity and wealth. Embrace Islam the supreme religion, faith, ideology and way of life with its unique ruling system, which is based on the principle that sovereignty and the supremacy belong to none but the almighty God and which protects the creed of man, his wealth, mind, honour, and the life of the people, regardless of their race, colour and origin.' [41]

The Queen needs our faithful support and regular prayers as the head of the Church of England, whether we are part of the Anglican denomination or another. The Bible is quite clear:

'Therefore I exhort first of all that supplications, prayers, intercessions, and giving of thanks be made for all men, for kings and all who are in authority, that we may lead a quiet and peaceable life in all godliness and reverence. For this is good and acceptable in the sight of God our Saviour, who desires all men to be saved and to come to the knowledge of the truth.'

(1 Timothy 2:1–4, NKJV)

It has been my privilege to pray in the Palace of Westminster on several occasions as an invited guest of one of the MPs. You do not need to be invited to enter the Houses of Parliament. You can go there and sit in the Strangers' Gallery of the House of Commons to watch debates, and likewise observe the proceedings in the House of Lords. I urge you to make a visit and, as you watch, to pray silently that our Christian heritage be maintained.

Prince Charles canvasses support for Islam

The Prince of Wales, our future king, who will be head of the Church of England one day, said that he would prefer to be called defender of faiths, rather than the defender of the faith –

Christianity. He told experts on the Middle East that 'Islam had retained a more integrated view of the world than materialistic Western society'. Speaking some time ago at Wilton Park, Steyning, West Sussex, and reported in the *Daily Telegraph* of 14 December 1996, Prince Charles suggested that employing more Muslim teachers would allow British children to learn from Islamic values. The article continues:

> 'It is not the first time that the prince, who is patron of the Oxford Centre for Islamic studies, has raised Islamic values.' [42]

Prince Charles thinks there is much to praise in Islam. He has held talks with one of the world's most influential Moslem leaders. A report states that 'his decision to receive the Sheik of Al-Azhar, the spiritual head of the Sunni Moslems, is said to underline his commitment to deepening his ties with Islam' [43] In another report in the *Daily Mail*:

> 'Charles who sometimes in private wears a Moslem djellaba (a long flowing Arabic garment) has been criticised by Christian groups for his failure to criticise Islamic human right abuses and persecution of Christians. At the end of the month he was to host a dinner at St. James Palace for the Oxford Centre for Islamic Studies, which has provoked powerful opposition to its plan to build a 108 foot minaret in the heart of the city.' [44]

Prince Charles has a duty to host important dignitaries, and when he does he should lobby for equal treatment being extended to the Christian faith.

Islam is an ideology that seeks power by any means possible, so it is easy to see how the Royal Family would be a target for Islamic influence. It is an open secret that not only does Islam want to convert ordinary folk, it also wants key leaders in Britain, even the Queen herself if possible! The Prime Minister and Members of Parliament, heads of industry, anyone with influence, are targets for Muslims to convert.

What other evidence is there of Judaeo-Christian values being eroded to the advantage of Islam? I can give you examples where this has already happened in schools and further education, town council resolutions, edicts preventing the celebration of Christmas and the establishment of Islamic banking.

There is a move to encourage pupils in schools to be exposed to the teachings of other faiths in multi-cultural Britain, particularly where Christian families are in the minority. Education Minister David Hall recently remarked:

> 'We think it is vital for Surrey pupils to be equipped to live in a multi-cultural, multi-faith world. Learning about a diversity of religions from a young age will teach pupils to respect and empathise with other cultures and at the same time ensure their awareness of the special place of Christianity within this country.' [45]

According to Mr Hall, everyone in Britain should understand the importance of learning from other people's cultures and way of life. If one religious group is in the minority in an area, they should not be deprived of their basic rights.

Christmas is one of the most important celebrations by Christians worldwide. As a country with the Judeo-Christian heritage everyone, adults and children, should have the right to celebrate this important Christian festival in Britain. However, exactly the opposite occurred in a school in Yorkshire. The *Daily Telegraph* of 22 August 1987 reported on a situation that had arisen in a school in the village of Thornhill Lees near Dewsbury, West Yorkshire. Some parents refused to send their children to a Church of England school where 93% of the pupils are Muslims.

One reason why they were angry was that the children would not be allowed to celebrate Christmas. One parent stated that 'the standard of education was not what the parents expected, and even though it is a Church school, morning prayers are not held and neither was Christmas celebrated. Two extra weeks were taken off school for other religious festivals.'

We are grateful for the religious freedom that we enjoy in this nation, which is extended to all people irrespective of their religious affiliation and ethnic origin, but this decision seems to contradict Christians' right to religious freedom. Would the same freedom be granted to Christians in Muslim nations like Saudi Arabia and Iran? I doubt very much that if the situation were reversed and there were a majority of children from Christian families attending a school in a Muslim nation they would ban all mention of Ramadan.

Bradford mosque

The city of Bradford has been benevolent towards the cause of Islam and has been described as being a trail-blazer in multi-cultural education. The town council even went as far as paying half the costs of a mosque built in the town after its first offer of a low interest loan was refused on the grounds that it was against Islamic principles to pay interest. I think the grant given by Bradford Council to build mosques is an extremely kind gesture! The question is whether this kind of gesture is reciprocal. Would Bradford Council grant equal money to Christians for maintenance of their places of worship? Furthermore, I wonder if the same gesture towards Christians would be reciprocated in a Muslim country. My church membership is mainly comprised of ethnic minorities. For many years we have found difficulty in finding a place to meet. I would love it if such benevolence as was afforded the Bradford Muslims was awarded to us from our local council!

Muslim prayers on the radio in Birmingham

Britain has a reputation for tolerance, which I think is widely appreciated. However, I think it is in danger of being too tolerant about Islam gaining ground to the extent that sometimes Muslims are given privileges that are denied to Christians. Consider this story by Aubrey Chalmers in the *Daily Mail* of December 1985:

> 'A mosque in a quiet city suburb is to summon Muslims to prayer in broadcasts said to be louder than a Concorde take-off ... Councillors have agreed to a month's trial during which the three-minute Arabic "calls" will boom from speakers on a minaret in Highgale, Birmingham, at noon and 3 p.m.'

The report says that Muslim leaders hope to reach up to 2,000 worshippers and eventually want permission for five daily messages, the first before dawn. The permission for the broadcast was granted by the city council's planning department.

St George's Day flag ban

Another demonstration of the influence of Islam in Britain occurred when Muslims in Luton objected to the council flying the flag of St George unless they could also fly a flag to mark the birthday of the Prophet Mohammed. According to the *Daily Mail*, 'The row blew up when Councillors in Luton, Beds voted to fly a flag over the town centre on St George's day, April 23, following suggestions from the public'. Some Muslims there hit the roof and, as the article continues, 'Labour Councillor Mohammed Ashraf said, "We would be offended if the council flies the flag of St George unless we can have a flag flying on the day of the birth of Mohammed." ' [46]

In 2004 the Red Cross December window displays were not

allowed to mention Christmas. Also in 2004 a competition to design a 'Christmas' card was held by Chichester College, an institution of adult education. The major entry criterion was that there should be no mention of Christmas on the card.

Islamic banking in Britain

The Qur'an (sura 2:278) states, 'O ye who believe! Fear God and give up what remains of your demand for usury, if you are indeed believers.' This phrase is interpreted that Muslims should not lend money to other Muslims and charge interest. Because of this, many Muslims are reluctant to use the High Street banks, preferring instead to use banks run by Muslims who use different principles in order to satisfy Shariah law. So-called Islamic banks are opening with increasing frequency in towns across the United Kingdom. One such bank is the Bank of Al Taqwa. This Bank advertises a capital of $50 million and advertises the following principles:

- Full adherence to Islamic law
- No restrictions for capital transfer (sic)
- Access to international markets
- Minimum tax levy on profit prior to distribution
- And no taxation on dividend

The HSBC, the second largest banking group in the world, launched Islamic banking in the UK recently, where loans can be granted to Muslims based on Islamic practices. This new HSBC Islamic banking is called the Amanah Bank Account. On their website the HSBC group explains how an Amanah Bank Account differs from their other Bank accounts. It states: 'An Amanah Bank Account from HSBC is designed to provide Shariah compliance so that you can carry out your day to day banking without having to compromise your deeply held principles.' [47]

Some of the promises made by HSBC to their customers on this account include:

1. They will not charge an overdraft review fee to customers who have not gone unintentionally overdrawn in the last six months.
2. 'We will waive overdraft review fees where you go overdrawn, by £10 or less.'

The Chancellor of the Exchequer, Gordon Brown, and the Inland Revenue have given special concessions to Muslims in different areas such as second marriages. I wonder whether people of other religious persuasions and backgrounds would consider this undue preferential treatment. Shouldn't the same treatment be meted out to Hindus, Buddhists and Christians? HSBC is not the only major High Street bank that has launched an Islamic banking product. On the 22 March 2005 Lloyds TSB launched Islamic home finance. A month earlier Lloyds TSB had launched an Islamic Current Account, which complies fully with Islamic Law (Shariah) which forbids both the payment and receipt of interest known as 'Riba'.

T. Levere writes in the *Guardian*:

> 'Banks meet the demands of UK's 1.8m Muslims. Islamic banking seems to have received a boost in the March 2005 budget when the chancellor pledged to "provide a level playing field for tax between equivalent financial products whether or not these involved the payment or receipt of interest".'[48]

I believe with the introduction of Islamic banking by two key players in the British banking industry, it is just a matter of time before others follow. The consequence will be significant as we see our High Streets with banks that comply with Shariah Law.

Conversions to Islam

There has been, and continues to be, an increase in conversions to Islam in Britain over the last couple of decades. In 1993, well over a decade ago, *The Times* newspaper reported that there were between 10,000 and 20,000 converts to Islam in Britain – the majority being women. 'The Muslim faith has many attractions to Western women.'[49]

> 'As the investigation in *The Times* on women and Islam has shown, the intellectual and moral certainty of this 1,400-year-old faith are proving attractive to many western women disillusioned with the moral relativity of their own culture. Though some are converting to Islam after marrying Muslim men, others are making the leap of faith as an independent act of spiritual self-improvement.'[50]

Such is the conversion to Islam in Britain that some have predicted that within the next decade or so, Islam will become a major force in British religion.

Another *Times* article concludes that, ' "within the next 20 years the number of British converts will equal or overtake the immigrant Muslim community that brought the faith here," says Rose Kendrick a religious education teacher at Hull Comprehensive and the author of a textbook guide to the Koran.'[51] It should be said that since this prediction was made over a decade ago, there has been a marked increase in converts to Islam in Britain. Can tens of thousands of conversions make a significant impact on close to sixty million? Britain has a declining and ageing population. We are a nation with a falling birth rate. On the other hand Islam is a religion that allows polygamy; men may marry as many as four women. Furthermore, Muslims tend to have many children. Conservative population statistics show that the Muslim world population is approximately 1.1 billion. They are increasing annually by about 34 million people. On average, every day, 100,000 children are born to Muslim parents. With declining births of non-Muslims and the greater birth rate of British Muslims, there will be a marked change in the demographics of society in Britain. Studies have shown that demographic change brings about changes in the needs of people. When there is an increase in the Muslim population of Britain there will be an increased demand for mosques and Muslim schools, Islamic centres and Quranic schools. It is not surprising that within the last decade mosques and Islamic centres have multiplied all over Britain, a trend that seems likely to continue.

Islamic influence in high places

Records show that not only are ordinary Britons converting to Islam, but prominent figures are also being converted to this fast growing religion. According to *The Times* several prominent converts to Islam include Matthew Wilkinson, a former head boy of Eton who studied at Cambridge University.[52] Gai Easton, a former British diplomat, now in his seventies is author of the book *Islam and the Destiny of Man*, required reading for bright young Anglo Saxons turning to his adopted faith. Nicholas Brandt, another Etonian and the son of an investment banker, swapped their destinies as sons of the establishment for a Slough semi shared with four other Muslims. The same article points to Lord Birt's son, Jonathan, 'who forsook a fast track into the ranks of the great and the good by converting in 1997 and starting a Ph.D. on British Islam. So did a son and a daughter of Lord Justice Scott, the scourge of Tory sleaze and the chairman of Arms to Iraq Inquiry'.[53]

Another prominent personality who converted to Islam is Jemima Khan, the daughter of the billionaire James Goldsmith, who married the former Pakistan cricket captain Imran Khan. A famous model, she must have influenced a large number of people in favour of Islam. What has been the appeal of Islam to some of these influential people who have converted? What will be the possible cumulative effect of Islam converting some strategic people? Like those in politics and government, successful businessmen and entrepreneurs are some of the power brokers in the nation. In Islam, religion and politics are inseparable, so when important political figures convert to Islam, that religion gains political power.

The post-9/11 era

In spite of the attack on the Twin Towers, Islam has actually made gains. Evidence suggests that there has been an upsurge in conversions and interest in Islam since the September 11 tragedy, especially among affluent young white Britons.

> 'Six months ago Elizabeth L. – a graduate in Political Science, the daughter of affluent white British parents, an opponent of terrorism in all its forms – climbed Mount Sinai at night to watch the desert sunrise from its summit. "It was the stillest, most peaceful place I have ever been," she says, "I could hear my feelings come up from within me, and in one surreal moment it all seemed to come together." '[54]

> 'Last Friday at 4.45pm, Elizabeth went to Regent's Park Mosque in Central London and converted to Islam. Why did she do this, many would have asked? Her remark was simple "Allah came knocking at my heart ... That's really how it feels. In many ways, it is beyond articulating, it's rather like falling in love." '[55]

Another high profile personality who has recently converted to Islam is Joe Dobson, son of the former Labour minister Frank Dobson, who believes that Islam transformed his spiritual life –

and helped him to get a first at University.[56] In the face of what many might have thought would be a damaging set-back, Islam post-9/11 is gaining ground.

Islam on the increase

Is Islam rapidly advancing in Britain? I believe there is evidence to show that it is. Many Church leaders would consider it alarmist to say that Islam is gaining ground in Britain. Many Christian leaders don't even consider militant Islam as a threat in Britain. I believe these leaders are either poorly informed or are refusing to face the facts. We can measure a steady growth in conversions to Islam in Britain over the last couple of decades including well educated women, a category that would at first seem unlikely to be attracted to that faith. What kind of influence does Islam have on our political terrain? Does Islam affect our policies, decisions, and decision makers? It's not just the ordinary folk on the street who are converted to Islam, the Prime Minister, Tony Blair, is having talks with leaders of the Muslim Community. Has Islam influenced our monarchy and the highest office in the land – the Prime Minister?

There is no doubt in my mind that Islam is exerting an increasing influence in Great Britain. What started as an insignificant trend is gradually becoming a force to be reckoned with in British religious and political life. Islam is gaining influence on all fronts. In banking, in education, politics and government, the media, the world of business, every area of life in Britain is moving towards positive discrimination in favour of Islam. Conversions to Islam by influential people are on the increase at the same time as church attendance is on the wane. Islam is having an ever-increasing access to the movers and shakers of our society. Islam is gaining ground in every walk of life. Muslims are becoming more vocal in their demands. I can see a distinct possibility that Islam might well become the dominant religion in the UK.

Some of the news is encouraging, that the government is considering expulsion of radical Muslim clerics, but we are being made aware by television and newspaper coverage that the Muslim community is active in seeking to share its opinions with the widest possible British audience.

Suggested practical action

▶ I encourage every Christian to befriend at least one Muslim family. We must remember that Muslims are not our enemy, Satan is. Jesus loves Muslims as He loves Christians, and died for the whole world.

▶ Rather than seeing Muslims as a threat, we should see their presence in our country as an evangelistic opportunity presented to us by God. Remember they are potential citizens of the kingdom of God.

▶ Because of the events that are happening right now, we should take the time to learn more from ministries with experience. I would encourage Christian leaders to study Islam and the Bible. Many Bible Colleges offer such a course. For further details contact us at World Harvest Christian Centre.

▶ I encourage Christians to peacefully protest by writing to their local council, County Council and MPs when Christians and Christian values are being marginalized.

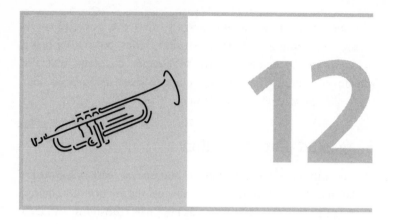

One Body

'That they all may be one; as thou, Father, art in me, and I in thee,
that they also may be one in us: that the world may believe that thou
hast sent me.'
(John 17:21, KJV)

As I look at Britain today, I see a fragmented Church. It's like the scattered remains after a bomb has gone off, or a plane accident. Here a hand, there a leg, bits missing, impossible to tell which bit came from which person. There has never been a time in our history when the prayer of Jesus in John 17 was more applicable. The Church I see today is a divided body, a Church that is not truly one. Most fellowships today have congregations based on racial, doctrinal or denominational differences.

Jesus prayed an important prayer to God for the Church on the night before He was betrayed, which has yet to be fulfilled, that the Church would be one. The Church that Jesus Christ, the chosen one, sent by the Father to be its everlasting head has a dismembered body. The true Church should not be divided based on race or ethnicity or colour. We should not even be divided because of our labels. The effectiveness of our 'gospel' is severely restricted by the existence of division. When the Church in a country speaks with one voice will be the time we see an unprecedented turning to God, a time of spiritual life like we have never known. The Church united will result in what I call oneness evangelism. The world will believe that God sent Jesus. Could the division in the Church be the reason why we are not experiencing the much-desired revival? Could the division of the Church be the reason why sinners are not taking the Church seriously?

> *'Sanctify them through thy truth: thy word is truth. As thou hast sent me into the world, even so have I also sent them into the world. And for their sakes I sanctify myself, that they also might be sanctified through the truth. Neither pray I for these alone, but for them also which shall believe on me through their word; That they all may be one; as thou, Father, art in me, and I in thee, that they also may be one in us: that the world may believe that thou hast sent me.'*
>
> (John 17:17–21, KJV)

> *'There is one body, and one Spirit, even as ye are called in one hope of your calling.'*
>
> (Ephesians 4:4, KJV)

> *'For we are members of his body, of his flesh, and of his bones.'*
>
> (Ephesians 5:30, KJV)

> *'For as the body is one, and hath many members, and all the members of that one body, being many, are one body: so also is Christ. For by one Spirit are we all baptised into one body, whether*

*we be Jews or Gentiles, whether we be bond or free; and have been
all made to drink into one Spirit.'*

(1 Corinthians 12:12–13, KJV)

*'But the natural man receiveth not the things of the Spirit of God:
for they are foolishness unto him: neither can he know them,
because they are spiritually discerned.'*

(1 Corinthians 2:14, KJV)

Only a truly spiritual person can receive the message of this
chapter. For some of you it will be as a leaping of a baby in the
womb, because you identify with the message. However, I know
that those who hold on to who they used to be before they met
Christ may find it a bitter pill to swallow.

I believe that the long-expected revival is coming! It will be
unparalleled in history. I believe with all my heart that the coming
revival will be unique. The manner, scope and the instruments of
the revival will surprise most of us. God wants to do something
very unusual in Great Britain. In the coming revival God wants to
make sure that no sector, denomination or leader takes any glory.
All the glory must go to Him alone. God wants to display the
glory and the uniqueness of His Body in the coming revival.

I believe that historically the Church in Britain has occupied a
very important position. The influence of Christianity brought by
the British has spread among the nations. From the time that the
British navy defeated the Spanish Armada in 1588, Britain became
the leading power on earth. Britain became Great Britain. In Queen
Victoria's day it was said that she ruled an empire on which the sun
never set. Everywhere the British went they built roads, railways
and schools. Officers imposed order, creating conditions highly
conducive to the spread of Protestant Christianity. Great Britain
brought the gospel to much of Asia, Africa and the Americas.

Today the tables are turned. Britain, which used to be a
missionary sending nation, has become a mission field. It is now

one of the darkest places spiritually on earth. God is not caught unawares. He has a plan for the redemption of Britain. And the instruments He will use are people who are the legacy of those glorious days of Empire. God's strategy is to bring back the fruits of the seeds that the British missionaries planted in different places. Within the last two decades there has been an influx of missionaries from former British colonies, all with one message on their lips: 'God told me to pack my luggage and come to Britain and He has promised that we are going to be part of the coming revival.'

I believe nothing happens by accident. God is a God of a plan; God is a God of purpose. Which members of the Church is God going to use to usher in the much-expected revival? I have often heard Christians declaring that God is going to use the 'black' churches, because of the fire of prayer that they carry. I don't believe the coming revival will come from the so-called 'black' church. Is the revival going to be spread by South Americans, or Asians? I don't think so.

What about the so-called 'white' church? One brother who wrote to me assured me that God was going to send the revival from the white church. Well dear brother, you may also be in for a big shock too. When God brings revival we will all be astounded because it will be unique. I believe it will be ushered in by the coming about of unity in the Church in Britain. God is waiting for us to establish unity so that He can fulfil His promise and pour out His blessing.

I believe that much that we do and say is hindering the move of the Spirit of God. The Church is being destroyed today because of 'lack of knowledge' (Hosea 4:6).

There is so much carnality in the Body of Christ that we need to repent of and get back to our first love. What do I mean by carnality? I mean doing things out of selfish or self-promoting motives, actions and thought patterns that are habitual without seeking the mind of the Spirit. I believe it's time we begin to align ourselves to what God is doing in Britain today. God intends to build one Church – the Body of Christ. This is why I believe that the coming revival will be different from anything we have seen before. How God will bring this about will be left to His Sovereignty. But all across this nation, right now, there are a handful of sentries watching and praying to see the Body of Christ emerge. This company is not going to accept anything less than one Body of Christ. They are not going to accept a divided, fragmented and dismembered body.

Metaphors for the Church

God gave to the apostle Paul a revelation of the Church that he described in several metaphors. Each of these analogies describes a special quality of the Church. Through the revelation that God gave to Paul, we know that the Church is first the assembly, second the household of God, third the Body of Christ and fourth and finally, the new man. This truth is mainly found in the Paul's epistle to the Ephesians.

The *ecclesia*, the Greek word used by Paul for the Church, means 'a group of people brought together, gathered together'. Some of our churches are like that, an assortment of strangers who enter a building once a week or less frequently who have little in common and who certainly do not share the same values or vision. Actually I have left out a most important point. The gathering together that Paul was describing was a gathering together for a common purpose. What was the common purpose of the early Church? Acts 2:42 gives us the answer. They met to listen to the teaching of the apostles, to share a meal including the Lord's Supper, and to pray. Acts also tells us that the believers had all things in common. They pooled their resources for the common good so there were no poor members in the early Church.

The household comprises an association of people and possessions. Some of the people are related to one another, the others are servants or slaves, or foreigners or tenants. I guess many of our churches would resemble this model.

The body metaphor is perhaps the highest analogy of the Church in the New Testament. For example in the household are the 'folks', while in the body are the members. When the folk of a household are happy and fulfilled they stay together but if unhappy they may separate from each another. Not so with the body. The body cannot separate parts without being severely disabled. Every part of a body has a useful function without which the other parts will suffer. The hand cannot say to the leg, 'I don't feel good about you so I will leave.' Neither can the eyes say to the ears, 'I do not feel good about you therefore I will leave.' Whether or not the eyes like the ears, they cannot depart from the body because their destinies are tied together. They are as they are because God has set them together. He's the one that sets us in the Body of Christ and He knows what is best for us. I see people deciding to leave one church and attend another just because they don't like something and have become offended, leaving what they call a 'white church' or what others call a 'black church' because they were mistreated. I believe this is wrong. Whether I am loved in a fellowship or not does not matter, my destiny is to be a member of the body.

In fact it is folly for a member of the body, whatever their colour, to mistreat another member of the same body. We have a term for such behaviour, we call it self-harm and realize this is a symptom of psychological disturbance because they inflict injury on themselves. Anyone can clearly see this is mad.

There's a lot of madness in the Body of Christ shown clearly by the way we treat other members of the Body. Across Britain today we see the Church divided. We have the 'white' church and the 'black' church; we have the church for the upper class, middle class, working class and the church for the no class! They don't mix. To give you an example, around 1948 there was a mass entry of brothers from the West Indies including Jamaica.

Many of them were Christian and came to Britain in the boat called the *Windrush*. These were brothers from the West Indies, not Jamaican brothers. There's a difference between the two. When these brothers and sisters went to their parish church some of them were shown the left foot of fellowship! Many of them were shown the door or told that the other members of the congregation would not be happy to welcome people of their colour. How shameful is that? What a disgrace to the cause of Christ! We were told by the missionaries that every man was of equal worth before God, and we believed it. Imagine our shock when we discovered we were treated in this shameful manner. When the time came for putting doctrine into practice, many failed woefully.

Certainly little has changed over fifty years. Many people still take pride in their race, nationality and class but these create false distinctions in the Body of Christ. Today you can see 'white' churches taking pride in being 'white'. Others take great pride in being 'black' – shown by the phrase 'black and proud'. This has done great damage to the work of God in Great Britain. While we should focus all our energies on fighting our common enemy, we are busy fighting each other. Some Caribbeans are still at loggerheads with the Africans for selling their ancestors into slavery. Some Caribbeans still hold grudges that the English did not receive them into fellowship when they came in the 1950s and 1960s. Yet all of us claim to be sons of God; we say we share the same Father. What a contradiction!

The new man

I'm sure most Christians will know 2 Corinthians 5:17:

> *'Therefore if any man be in Christ, he is a new creature: old things are passed away; behold, all things are become new.'*

(KJV)

What this scripture says is that once we are in Christ all things become new. We are a new creation; new species. However, the verse before is just as important:

> *'Wherefore henceforth know we no man after the flesh: yea, though we have known Christ after the flesh, yet now henceforth know we him no more.'*
>
> (2 Corinthians 5:16, KJV)

This scripture is very profound. As believers, new creatures in Christ Jesus, we have a new identity, and we are never to know any member of the Body of Christ after the flesh. This is why it is wrong to know me as a black person or as a Nigerian. I am a new creature; I am a citizen of heaven. Is that not what the Bible says?

> *'For our citizenship is in heaven, from which we also eagerly wait for the Saviour, the Lord Jesus Christ.'*
>
> (Philippians 3:20, NKJV)

The apostle Peter also declares our new found identity when we come to Christ:

> *'But ye are a chosen generation, a royal priesthood, an holy nation, a peculiar people; that ye should shew forth the praises of him who hath called you out of darkness into his marvellous light.'*
>
> (1 Peter 2:9, KJV)

Notice what Peter calls our nationality – a holy nation. I belong to the holy nation. My primary allegiance is not to Nigeria nor to the United Kingdom, but to the holy nation. This is why wherever I go I look for fellow citizens – their background, sex or the colour of their skin does not matter. This is the reason why

I refuse to be called a black or Nigerian pastor – I am not. My identity is a citizen of the holy nation, a son of God, a joint heir with Christ, Hallelujah!

Paul said he renounced everything he had put his confidence in before he met Christ. Before Paul's dramatic conversion he was a Jew, an educated theologian, a Pharisee. He was given the mandate by the Sanhedrin to persecute members of the young Church who the Sanhedrin thought were a blasphemous renegade sect, causing trouble. One of the observers of Stephen's death was Saul. Not only was Paul a Jewish theologian of high standing, he was also a Roman citizen by birth.

Let's consider what Paul wrote:

> *'For we are the circumcision, which worship God in the spirit, and rejoice in Christ Jesus, and have no confidence in the flesh. Though I might also have confidence in the flesh. If any other man thinketh that he hath whereof he might trust in the flesh, I more.'*
>
> (Philippians 3:3–4, KJV)

Notice what Paul is saying, that as those who have been circumcised in our hearts, we no longer place our confidence in the flesh. He goes further to state that if anyone had reason to glory or trust in the flesh, he had:

> *'Circumcised the eighth day, of the stock of Israel, of the tribe of Benjamin, an Hebrew of the Hebrews; as touching the law, a Pharisee; concerning zeal, persecuting the church; touching the righteousness which is in the law, blameless.'*
>
> (Philippians 3:5–6, KJV)

Notice what Paul says about the flesh. He is writing about physical and spiritual reasons to take pride in, to 'glory in the flesh' including his nationality, lineage and class:

'But what things were gain to me, those I counted loss for Christ.
Yea doubtless, and I count all things but loss for the excellency of the
knowledge of Christ Jesus my Lord: for whom I have suffered the loss
of all things, and do count them but dung, that I may win Christ.'
(Philippians 3:7–8, KJV)

Am I telling you to renounce your earthly nationality? Yes and
no. Yes, because we are new creatures, and we now belong to
another nation – a nationality that is far better than any on earth.
It is not right to relate to a fellow-believer based on who they used
to be before they met Christ. No, because when we are dealing
with those who are not Christians, or we find ourselves in
situations that will help the cause of the kingdom, then by all
means use it. That was precisely what Paul did in Acts 25. You
never see him identifying believers based on their nationality or
race, but as the Christians meeting together at a certain place.
When writing to encourage them he would write to the saints
who are in Corinth or Ephesus or Rome. He identified them
based on their new identity. When we become new creatures,
our communication has to change because of the revelation we
now have from the Holy Spirit. A divided body can never
function properly. A divided and dismembered body is sick. And
a sick body is not going to win many battles.

'But now in Christ Jesus, you who once were [so] far away,
through (by, in) the blood of Christ have been brought near. For He
is [Himself] our peace – our bond of unity and harmony. He has
made us both [Jew and Gentile] one (body), and has broken down
(destroyed, abolished) the hostile dividing wall between us.'
(Ephesians 2:13–14, Amplified)

'Put off your old nature which belongs to your former manner of
life and is corrupt through deceitful lusts.'
(Ephesians 4:22, RSV)

One of the truths that God is trying to bring to His Body in the United Kingdom is the revelation of the one new man. To understand the revelation of the one new man we must first understand our original position. We are descended from Adam. Under the dispensation of the old man, Adam was the original common ancestor, the head of the family. We must also note that in Adam humanity was divided, from the time of Genesis to the birth of the Church. The story of humanity according to the fleshly inheritance is the story of division. However, what was divided in Adam was brought together in the new man. In the new man we are made one.

The Holy Spirit, through the teaching of the apostle Paul, gave the revelation of the new man. Those of us who were once far off from God, and from one another, have been brought together in Christ Jesus. Believers from different backgrounds and colour have now been brought near through the work of the cross. Furthermore, Jesus Christ has broken down the middle wall of partition; He has brought together Jews and Gentiles into one body. This is why it is wrong for anyone to refer to any person or church as being Jewish or Gentile. I used to be a Gentile, but now I am not a Gentile, I belong to the holy race. I belong to the Church of Christ, in which there's no place for Jews or Gentiles. Paul counsels believers to put off the old man and put on the new man. It is a walk of faith and it requires the renewing of our minds. As our minds become renewed, our language begins to change. We begin to use new words from the Holy Spirit.

Let me clarify this issue. Colossians 3:10–11 says:

> *'And have put on the new man, which is renewed in knowledge after the image of him that created him: where there is neither Greek nor Jew, circumcision nor uncircumcision, Barbarian, Scythian, bond nor free: but Christ is all, and in all.'*

(KJV)

In the new man, according to Paul in this passage, there is neither Greek nor Jew, circumcision nor uncircumcision, barbarian, Scythian, bond nor free ... Take note of the word, neither, not either. In order words you can't pick and choose. Neither means none of the above.

There's no place in the new man for the Jew or Gentile, there's no place for the black person or the white person, there's no place for the British or the African, there's no place for the Jamaican or the Irish. There's no place for separation in the new man, because Christ is all and in you all. There's no natural person in the new man. There's no room for any natural person. In the new man there is room for only one person – Christ! He is all the members of the new man and in all the members. By the mouth of two or more witnesses every truth will be established. Let's look at Galatians 3:27–28:

> *'For as many of you as have been baptised into Christ have put on Christ. There is neither Jew nor Greek, there is neither bond or free, there is neither male nor female: for ye are all one in Christ Jesus.'*
> (KJV)

> *'For by one Spirit are we all baptised into one body, whether we be Jews or Gentiles, whether we be bond or free; and have been all made to drink into one Spirit.'*
> (1 Corinthians 12:13, KJV)

One of the ministries of the Holy Spirit is to baptise us into the Body of Christ. Brothers who used to pride themselves as white believers have been baptised into the same body as those with black skin. The 'Chinese' brother has also been baptised into the same body. I am excited about this truth. There are still some believers who take pride in who they used to be and this does not help the cause of Christ. I was born and raised in the nation of Nigeria, in West Africa. I have a dark skin. Over thirteen years ago, God spoke to me to move to the UK because He was going to use me to be part of the army that would see a great revival in the country and usher in the second coming of Jesus.

The natural thing for me to do would be to look around for Nigerians or Africans and align myself with them. I don't have anything against anyone doing just that, it is just that my vision and walk with God is different. It would be the easiest thing to hang around the Pastors' fraternity from Africa but because I have caught the revelation of the one new man, because I can see what God is about to do, I have to make sure that I see the vision of the one new man fulfilled. It is a work of the Spirit. I don't see a believer from the natural perspective, I don't relate to believers based on their race or nationality. What I am relating to is Christ in them.

If only the Church in Great Britain would see the vision of the new man, all divisions would be gone. I know that there are many Christians who would describe themselves as Spirit-filled and believe in the Bible as being sufficient for doctrine – yet they are unable to fellowship with people of different skin colour or class. I have worked in the UK as a minister for over thirteen years. I know there's a lot of repenting that must be done in this area. You see some believers who never fellowship with any brother with a dark skin. In fact there are some who will never submit to the leadership of a 'black' pastor. Away with those fleshy attitudes! Away with that arrogance and pride! I say away with racism in the Body of Christ!

It's not just white believers who have a problem. There are many 'black' Christian workers who God has sent to Britain hindering the move of God's Spirit. Many have a ghetto mentality. Many will not let go of their blackness, even in the face of the revelation of God's Word. I believe God is going to leave out many people in the coming revival, some of them prominent leaders who know better, but have been caught in the hypocrisy of Peter (see Galatians 2:12).

When to use your natural identity

'What's wrong with identifying myself as Nigerian or British when I'm a believer?' you may well ask, or 'Under what conditions should I be using my earthly nationality?'

Obviously if a government or bank official asks to see your passport as proof of identity you will show it to them. Also we should use our original nationality when talking with people who are not Christians, dealing with people who are not believers. We are in the world, but not of the world. As people who have dual citizenship when we deal with the state or its representatives we must give unto Caesar the things that are Caesar's and unto God the things that are God's.

In Acts 22, when Paul was standing in defence of his ministry, he began to recount his ministry. We are told in this chapter that his audience lifted up their voices in anger and they were about to lynch him. The chief captain, however, rescued him and asked for him to be brought into the castle and scourged – in other words Paul was about to be punished without being found guilty, which was contrary to Roman law.

> *'And they gave him audience unto this word, and then lifted up their voices, and said, Away with such a fellow from the earth: for it is not fit that he should live. And as they cried out, and cast off their clothes, and threw dust into the air, the chief captain commanded him to be brought into the castle, and bade that he should be examined by scourging; that he might know wherefore they cried so against him.*
>
> *And as they bound him with thongs, Paul said unto the centurion that stood by, Is it lawful for you to scourge a man that is a Roman, and uncondemned?*
>
> *When the centurion heard that, he went and told the chief captain, saying, Take heed what thou doest: for this man is a Roman.'*
> (Acts 22:22–26, KJV)

Look at the wisdom of Paul. He was about to be punished
without having committed any offence at all. As soon as he
mentioned he was a Roman citizen the attitude of the authorities
changed. They released him immediately. Later on when taken
into custody again he used the same identity to be taken to Rome
for trial rather than suffer summary justice from corrupt local
officials.

Dry bones

As I look around me I see in dry bones everywhere, a body that
has been cut asunder, a dismembered body. The 'whites' are
divided from the 'blacks', the middle class separated from the
working class, the 'Caribbeans' from the English – yet they are all
supposed to be members of one body, the Church. Everybody
is going their own way, doing their own thing. The situation
seems hopeless. The Body of Christ in Great Britain is just like
the picture of Ezekiel. In Ezekiel 37 God took the prophet to the
valley of dry bones. Here God showed the prophet what used to
be an exceedingly great army. Now it was reduced to loose bones,
not a shred of flesh left, not even a meal for a mouse.

> '*And he said unto me, Son of man, can these bones live? And I
> answered, O Lord GOD, thou knowest.*
>
> *Again he said unto me, Prophesy upon these bones, and say unto
> them, O ye dry bones, hear the word of the LORD. Thus saith the
> Lord GOD unto these bones; Behold, I will cause breath to enter into
> you, and ye shall live: And I will lay sinews upon you, and will
> bring up flesh upon you, and cover you with skin, and put breath in
> you, and ye shall live; and ye shall know that I am the LORD.*'
>
> (Ezekiel 37:3–6, KJV)

As Ezekiel watched, the bones were covered with tendons, the
joints re-established and the decaying process was reversed until

the bodies were complete. A second prophecy from the obedient Ezekiel and the army stood to attention ready for battle.

> '*Then he said unto me, Son of man, these bones are the whole house of Israel: behold, they say, Our bones are dried, and our hope is lost: we are cut off for our parts.*'
>
> (Ezekiel 37:11, KJV)

What is interesting from this situation is that as the prophet spoke the dismembered collection of old bones began to come together – the bones came together, bone to his bone! Hallelujah! This is what I see happen all across the British Isles. As the Spirit of God begins to move powerfully like a rushing mighty wind, as we begin to speak as we are commanded, speaking the very words of God, we will begin to see a divided, dismembered Church coming together, bone to bone! We will begin to see a coming together of the Church in Britain, like never before. We will begin to see barriers, artificial, fleshly barriers coming down and Jesus being exalted and glorified.

As a member of the Body begin to speak out the Word of the Lord to His Church. It's a new day. You will start to see a very different Church emerging. This is why I challenge the Church. I challenge all believers, all Christians across this land to wake up. Wake up! Rise up out of carnality and division that we have been slumbering in over the last couple of decades. Start to embrace what God is bringing about! Let the Church arise for a new day is dawning.

Suggested practical action

▶ I encourage Christians to begin to change the way they talk about other Christians. For example, to use labels such as the 'black church' or the 'white church' is wrong, since in Christ we all belong to the same Church.

► Church leaders especially I exhort to set an example in embracing believers from all backgrounds and begin to have regular meetings with others of different background.

► Let's begin to speak against everything that tries to divide the Body of Christ in this nation along ethnic, denominational or racial lines.

► Read two important books, *The Elimination of Erroneous Distinctions in the Body of Christ* and *The New Man*, both by Bishop Robert E. Smith, published by Total Outreach for Christ Ministries Inc., Little Rock, Arkansas. You can order copies from your local Christian Bookstore or by phoning World Harvest Church office on 0207 358 8080.

Persecution is Nearer than You Think

'Then you will be handed over to be persecuted and put to death, and you will be hated by all nations because of me.'
(Matthew 24:9, NIV)

As I said in my first book *Great Britain Has Fallen*, I was born, raised and spent the greater part of my youth in Nigeria, a member of the Commonwealth. I came to the United Kingdom as a missionary in the summer of 1992. Before I came I studied the spiritual history of the country I would be living in. I familiarized myself with biographies of men and women like Charles Spurgeon, Evan Roberts, John Knox, William Wilberforce, Elizabeth Fry, Hannah Moore, Florence Nightingale, John Newton, John and Charles Wesley, Isaac Newton and others. According to my research not only did we adopt Christianity as a state religion, but also the very fabric of British society is based on Christian principles. They include our legal system. Social security, financial structure, media, architecture and education were all based on Christian principles.

When I write about persecution in Britain, it comes from this background that Christianity is at the heart of all our way of life. At present Church and state are interlinked. Our monarch is head of state; she is also head of the Church of England. At her coronation over fifty years ago, Queen Elizabeth II swore before 27 million people that she would 'To the utmost of her power maintain the laws of God, the true profession of the gospel and the Protestant reformed religion established by law'. She also promised to 'preserve unto the bishops and clergy of this realm, and to the churches committed to their charge all such rights and privileges as by law do or shall appertain to them'. It is from this Christian perspective that I want this chapter to be understood.

My research into the origins of the Christian faith and its impact on Britain was both encouraging and disturbing. The first time the British Isles came into contact with Christianity was around 596–597 when Augustine came to this island, but there are some who argue for a much earlier date, coinciding with the Roman Conquest of Britain around AD 43 or earlier. Some claim that Paul set foot in this country. Probably there was some spread of the gospel by the efforts of individuals whose names we lack, since there was certainly evidence of the Celts adopting Christianity before Augustine arrived. Gildas, a Celtic priest and one of the earliest historians on the conquest of Britain, claims that Britain received the gospel in the latter part of the reign of the Emperor Tiberius. This was around AD 14–37. The effect of the early contact was that our ancestors embraced Christianity which became the state religion by the Middle Ages.

The history of the early Church was one of persecution after it was decided that it was not an insignificant sect of Judaism, which enjoyed *religio licita* (allowed religious practice) status under

Roman occupation. The first Christian martyrs refused to join in worship of the Roman Emperor who declared himself to be divine! Jesus prophesied His return to earth before He ascended into heaven, and that we were to expect certain conditions to be the sign of His imminent return. One of these conditions is an increase of persecution of Christians. He said the only reason why we would be maligned and hated by all peoples was for no other reason than that we are associated with Him.

Paul the apostle picks up the same theme, when he wrote in 2 Timothy 3:12 that *'In fact, everyone who wants to live a godly life in Christ Jesus will be persecuted'* (NIV). In other words, the fact that we base all our behaviour on the Word of God is an open invitation to persecution. Declaring certain practice to be sin according to the Christian faith is enough to qualify for sanctions in some quarters.

The history of the early Church confirms this. Because they preached the unadulterated gospel and declared that Jesus and not Caesar was Lord, and that salvation was found in none other than in Christ Jesus, they were hunted down, jailed, beaten, sawn into two, or were killed in public contests with wild animals. The Emperor Nero is said to have used human torches. Letters from prison by early bishops to their churches warned them to stay faithful in spite of persecution which should not be counted as something strange. As Christians we should prepare ourselves to suffer just as our Lord did. We have been called not just to believe in His name, but also to suffer on His behalf.

In the United Kingdom Christian persecution includes legal and institutional discrimination, sometimes formally enshrined in law, but also more subtle means such as poorer job or promotion prospects that are hard to substantiate. Persecution has already started and may well be intensified in the coming days. I want you to be aware of some of the snares, *'lest Satan should take advantage of us; for we are not ignorant of his devices'* (2 Corinthians 2:11, NKJV).

Street preacher arrested in Bournemouth for speaking out against homosexuality

One of the areas where Christians in the United Kingdom are likely to encounter persecution in the coming days is in the area of human sexuality, particularly homosexuality. The argument simply boils down to whether or not homosexual behaviour is compatible with Christian teaching. Is there anything really wrong in two men or two women having a sexual relationship when they both love each other? Some people don't see anything wrong in practising homosexuality; many Christians see it as a perversion.

Leviticus chapters 18 and 20 set out clearly the types of sexual relationships that God approves of and those that must be avoided.

> *'Homosexuality is absolutely forbidden.'*
>
> (Leviticus 18:22, Living)

The problem comes for us when we encounter someone who says they are a homosexual. Some preachers encourage their listeners or audience to renounce this lifestyle, turn to Jesus and receive salvation for their soul. This is exactly what a sixty-seven-year-old pensioner John Hammond of Bournemouth did, when he turned up in the city centre with a placard that stated 'Stop Immorality, Stop Homosexuality. Jesus Gives Peace'. Mr Hammond was soon surrounded by gay rights protestors who pelted him with mud and water. He was knocked to the ground. The police intervened and arrested him. He was charged with an offence under Section 5 of the Public Order Act, 1986. It was said that on 13 October 2001, he was in the square in Bournemouth when he displayed writing or sign which was threatening, abusive or insulting, within the hearing or sight of a person likely to be caused harassment, alarm or distress thereby, and that this was contrary to Sections 5(1) and 5(6) of the 1986 Act.

Mr Hammond was subsequently found guilty in the courts,

and sent to prison. He died while serving his sentence. The facts of this case give rise to some fundamental issues. There are only two places in Britain where the absolute right of free speech is allowed. One is Speakers' Corner in Hyde Park, London; the other is the floor of the Houses of Parliament. Those who wish to exercise their freedom of expression can do so without committing any offence as long as they so within the law. The second issue is the difficult question of how far freedom of speech or behaviour must be limited in the general public interest. Mr Hammond was expressing his rights within the confines of the law. This case raises serious questions about our evangelistic practices. Are we going to be allowed to preach the gospel freely or are our forces of law going to use this case to curtail our efforts? How far can preachers go today? Will preachers be allowed to express their interpretation of Leviticus 19:22 on TV or would this view be censored? It is only a matter of time before a preacher, particularly one who preaches the uncompromising Word of God, will be on trial because someone in their congregation was offended by what they said.

Sex-change pastor sues Christian centre

Recently the Gender Recognition Bill was being debated in Parliament. This raised an outcry from the Christian community because of its far-reaching implication. What is the Gender Recognition Bill about? It is about the status of people who wish to officially change their gender. Simply put it allows a man to become a woman in law and then to marry another man. Similarly a woman can become a man and marry a woman. In either case from an orthodox Christian perspective it remains a same-sex relationship.

Under this bill churches have already been threatened with legal action. The Christian Institute, one of the foremost voices in defending the Christian faith in the public arena, has highlighted some of the cases where churches have been taken to court. The most prominent case was that of the pastor and members of the Vine Christian Centre, South Wales who were sued after a man who had a 'sex change' was told he could not attend the 'Ladies' Prayer Meeting or use the ladies' toilets. According to the report the church had shown considerable patience and compassion towards the man (he had been attending for two years) but refused to treat him as a woman. The article continues – that the members were advised by their lawyer that defending the case through the courts could be very expensive, which made them discuss the possibility of having to sell the church building to pay. This reveals the price the fellowship and other churches may have to pay for defending the truth.

When the Gender Recognition Bill was taken to the House of Lords, three Bishops voted against the proposal championed by Baroness O'Cathain. They were the Bishops of Manchester, Newcastle and Worcester. The Bishop of Winchester spoke against it before abstaining. The amendment was narrowly defeated in the House of the Lords by just five votes.[57] I find it very difficult to accept that someone in a position of spiritual oversight, a bishop of the Church of England, who I would expect to defend the Bible, would vote against or abstain in this situation. This would never happen in Africa! This shows how far some ecclesiastical authority has become debased.

Persecution of Christians in the Health Service

Christians can and are being penalized for standing by their Christian convictions. A junior doctor, Dr Everett Taylor, claims that he was discriminated against in a job application because he refused to take part in abortions. He is calling on the National Health Service to stop discriminating against religious beliefs. He was told that his stance on abortion let him down at the interview with the North Glasgow University's Hospital Trust. After the interview he was told that he would not be given one of the twelve available posts because of his answer.[58]

Hull Christian Union banned for being run by Christians

In another show of political correctness, student chiefs at Hull University have threatened to ban a Christian Union (CU) because it doesn't allow non-believers such as atheists to run the student society. The Constitution of the CU requires members of its executive committee to be practising Christians who must sign the CU's basis of faith. This was just too much for the Student Union Council, which has threatened to revoke the CU's status as a Union Society unless the CU changes its Constitution to allow non-Christian students into the CU leadership. It claims the CU's Constitution is 'discriminatory'. Commenting on this saga, Colin Hart, Director of The Christian Institute, said; 'It is completely crazy. Hull CU is being told that it cannot require its leaders to be Christians. It is totally intolerant of the right of students to associate with like-minded people ... The decision of the Union is totally unlawful.'[59] I wholeheartedly agree with Mr Hart. It is an insult to the Christian Union. I don't think they would consider trying to ban Muslims from running an Islamic Society.

Warwick Student Union Council recently voted to disaffiliate the Christian Union because of its view on homosexuality. The Christian Union cannot now operate from the Student Union building or use its facilities.[60]

Christianity easy target for satire

In the entrance hall of the BBC an inscription says: 'To Almighty God. This shrine of arts, music and literature is dedicated by the First Governors in the year of our Lord 1931, John Reith being

Director General. It is their prayer that good seed sown will produce a good harvest, that everything offensive to decency and hostile to peace will be expelled and that the nation will incline its ear to those things which are lovely, pure and of good report and thus pursue the path wisdom and virtue.'

In spite of their promise the BBC, invoking their duty to counterbalance any opinion, end up by diluting and refuting their original Christian stance. Now it seems Christianity is fair game for comedians. According to Lord Dubbs, Chairman of the Broadcasting Standard Commission, comedians and dramatists delight in 'pouring scorn' on Christianity but are 'timid' about knocking Muslims. He said that 'Islam was accorded far more respect on television and radio than other religions because satirists were "cautious" and "self-censoring" when faced with the prospect of causing offence to Muslims.' He goes further to remark that 'in portraying Muslims they have held back; they have censored themselves, they are timid. I have seen them pour scorn on Christianity more than other religions. Christianity is an easier and more acceptable target...' He admitted that the BBC had also shown bias in favour of Muslims. 'We have tried to treat the religions equally. I doubt we have succeeded. I think we have shaded a bit on the side of Islam.' [61] I wholeheartedly agree with Lord Dubbs in his observation. I was speaking with a journalist recently and he remarked that one thing all media houses seem to be agreed upon is to leave Islam alone. In a so-called 'Christian' country we respect and honour Islam far more than we honour Christianity. How are the mighty fallen, O Great Britain!

Mocking Christ makes movies

No religious leader comes under mockery in films as much as Christ. For example in 1999 a film called *Dogma* presented a satire on religion, which featured a descendant of Jesus working in an abortion clinic and a pop singer in the role of God. It also depicts Joseph and Mary having sex. The film was produced by Miramax, a subsidiary of Disney.[62] I wonder if they will ever dare depict Mohammad in the same manner. I am certain that they will not attempt this!

The Jerry Springer Opera

In January 2005 the BBC not only breached its own guidelines for decency and good taste, but it insulted Britain's Christian community by showing *Jerry Springer, the Opera*. The show was not only blasphemous, but it was obscene. In it Jesus was portrayed as an overweight, half-dressed homosexual. The show was filled with swear words. Even Jerry Springer himself said in a radio interview he was glad his mother was no longer living because she would not have liked his programmes. Condemning the BBC's decision for broadcasting the programme, Councillor Alan Craig, the Leader of the Christian Peoples Alliance Party, remarked:

> 'The BBC would not dare to treat Mohammad in this insulting way. Christians do not expect a public service broadcaster funded by their licence fee to mock Jesus Christ like this. The actions of the BBC show that stronger control is needed and this must be brought up during the Royal Charter renewal process . . .' [63]

Serious Organized Crime and Police Bill

Perhaps what will be considered the greatest threat to religious liberty is the Serious Organized Crime and Police Bill, Clause 119, which is being debated in Parliament as I write. A new crime of incitement to religious hatred would be created by amending the existing law against the incitement to racial hatred in the Public

Order Act 1986. It is proposed that where the existing law reads 'racial hatred', the new law will read 'racial or religious hatred' and that religious hatred will be defined as 'hatred against a group of persons defined by reference to religious belief or lack of religious belief'. The key problem in this new bill is that one could be criminalized if one's communication or actions are deemed 'threatening, abusive or insulting'. Not the least of the problems this rewording will cause is that it will make critical debate almost impossible. At the moment I don't believe Christians generally understand how dangerous passing this law will be.

It's happening in Australia

On 17 December 2004 two Christian pastors in Australia were found guilty of 'religious vilification' because they criticized Islam. A court in the Southern Australian state of Victoria found that the two pastors had breached Section 8 of the Racial and Religious Tolerance Act 2001 which bans conduct which 'incites hatred'. A case was brought against the two pastors, following comments made by them in a church seminar in March 2002. The comments included drawing attention to the teaching of the Qur'an and questioning Islam's compatibility with Western democracy. Shortly after the seminar the Islamic Council of Victoria filed a legal action against the pastors.[64] At the moment, the pastors are waiting to be sentenced. Could this not set a major precedent?

It's also happening in Sweden

Another reason why Christians in Britain must take the Incitement to Religious Hatred Bill seriously is because of what is happening in other countries. In Sweden, Pastor Ake Green, was recently sentenced to prison for preaching a sermon on homosexuality. This took place early in 2005.[65]

What people have said about the incitement offence

'Most organized religions claim that they have an exclusive truth that has been given to them. They usually say some pretty harsh things about other religions and there is a genuine danger that if one reads religious tracts one will find many reasons in the Bill to prosecute people for their religious beliefs.'

(John Owen Jones MP – Labour)

'The Religious Incitement Measures will damage freedom of expression and religious liberty. They will prevent fair comment about religious beliefs and cults and enable them to silence their critics ... Some cults are corrosive to society, especially Christian society, which is still broadly the society that we enjoy in this country – and I do not want everyone ever to be at risk of being prosecuted for saying that.'

(Bob Spink MP – Conservative)

'If we are free to adopt a religion we must also be free to discuss the danger of other religious beliefs.' [66]

'IHRC would like to express its deep concern at Home Secretary David Blunkett's latest proposals to outlaw incitement to religious hatred. Rather than enjoying additional protection from the law, religious minorities could find themselves the targets of prosecutions under the proposed legislation.' [67]

'The difficulties of legislating religious hatred as an extra ground for prosecutors are enormous. The issue is not that we should be tolerant of all religions and all adherents of different religions, but whether religious hatred as such can be identified as a category on which prosecutions can be based. We have laws against inciting racial hatred, and indeed incitement to violence on any grounds. Why do we need to add religious hatred?'[68]

As stated earlier, I believe if the Incitement to Religious Hatred Bill becomes law it will have unprecedented consequences to the spread of the gospel of Christ in Great Britain. I envisage the possibility of many Christian leaders being taken to court and even facing imprisonment.

What is more crucial is that Christian persecution in Britain will be enshrined in law. I see laws being passed in Parliament that will inevitably contradict basic religious freedom, which was only established after lengthy see-sawing between Catholics and Protestants, Church of England and Non-Conformists. The right to discuss religion is a fundamental human right that is now under threat. I also see religious pressure coming from European legislation. I fear European laws may well encroach on our freedom of speech causing yet further restriction on what we may say. The person of Christ and His message will come under major attack in the coming days. Those that stand up and defend the claims of Christ as the only true way may end up ostracized, castigated, and ridiculed!

I predict that homosexual activists will become even more influential, and there will be cases of Christians defending the Bible in the courts! This could have an unexpected benefit in that Christians of differing denominations will be forced to unite and speak with one voice. It will become obvious to all Christians that we belong to one Body in Christ. In the meantime we need to get ready for what is coming. This is the time for leaders to prepare and equip the saints; it is time to wake up to reality.

This is the day to stand up for what we believe. It is our time to defend the faith.

Suggested practical action

▶ Inform yourself of places where Christians are being imprisoned for their faith or being killed for their faith by subscribing to a newsletter from a reputable Christian organization such as Open Doors.

▶ Commit to regular prayer for one of those countries, either on your own or with others of like mind.

▶ Pray for those who persecute you, pray for blessing to come to them and look to God to right any wrong you personally may feel has been done to you. Remember God can make even your enemies to be at peace with you when your way pleases the Lord.

▶ Alert your church leader if you encounter religious prejudice and ask for the church to pray.

▶ I urge church leaders to contact the Association of Christian Lawyers for information regarding proposed legislation that may be prejudicial to Christians.

▶ Urge the Evangelical Alliance to do more to support Christians who are facing persecution for their faith.

What Can I Do?

'Faith by itself, if it is not accompanied by action, is dead.'
(James 2:17, NIV)

The whole purpose of the watchman signalling to the city to wake up was a call to action. Each person had their allotted task to which the trumpet call was the signal to act. I believe we have had a strong clear sound from the trumpet and now is the time to fulfil our destiny in making Britain a place where Christian standards and the freedom to preach the gospel is maintained.

The first task all of us must do is pray, pray and pray again. All through this book I have been impressed strongly with the need for the whole body to join together and pray. When we pray it allows us to perceive what the Spirit is saying to us, the Church. We may need to repent for our own sin in order for the eyes of our understanding to be opened. We may well need to repent on behalf of this nation for some of the legislation passed that comes from a humanist agenda. We certainly need to pray, in the light of the recent London bombings, that legislation proposed in order to protect us is not at the same time returning the UK to curtail some of the religious freedom that was won in this country over the centuries since Henry VIII.

I believe the call to prayer and the call to action are one and the same. In everything we do, prayer is not an optional extra, it is the essential eternal obligation and privilege of every Christian to enter boldly into God's presence to find grace for help in time of need. Today our Christian heritage is in danger of being superseded and so now is the time for us to take the baton in the race of faith and run our lap.

There are many ways to pray. Ask the Holy Spirit to guide you and teach you to pray. You can expect fresh meaning as you read through familiar Bible passages on prayer. You can expect to be thrilled with seeing positive answers as you pray. I urge you to make a regular commitment to be at the prayer meeting in your church. Familiarize yourself with current events and ask for guidance from the Holy Spirit as to how and what to pray. You may find yourself declaring boldly to the principalities and powers the Word of the Lord. You may find yourself weeping. Do not be surprised, God is never too busy to hear your prayers.

'The prayer of a righteous man [or woman] *is powerful and effective.'*

(James 5:16b, NIV)

Postscript

The alarm has already gone off; the whistle has been blown; the wake-up call has been sounded and a new level of spiritual prayer warfare hitherto unknown in the history of Great Britain has commenced!

I had nearly finished the writing of this book and the manuscript was being edited when the first wave of terrorist bombs went off in several places in London on July 7th 2005. As you already know, many lives were destroyed, others were wounded and still many more are nursing the emotional trauma and scars of this incident. As I write, the government is taking some drastic measures that will change our lifestyle and which I believe will have greater consequences in the days ahead.

July 7th was certainly a wake-up call. It was a wake-up call for the nation to be vigilant, but more importantly for the Church. I believe what happened on the streets of London was a visible sign of the spiritual onslaught that is going on in the spiritual realm. It was but a microcosm of the warfare the enemy, Satan, has declared in the spirit! How are we to respond to the situation? I believe the prophet Joel has given us a word of instruction in the practical steps or actions we can take. He says,

> 'Consecrate a fast,
> Call a sacred assembly;
> Gather the elders
> And all the inhabitants of the land

Into the house of the LORD *your God,*
And cry out to the LORD*.'*

(Joel 1:14, NKJV)

While the forces of law and order are hunting for the planners of these attacks and our government is busy debating what new measures the nation needs to secure our borders, God is calling for a solemn assembly where the Church will wait on God with fasting and repentance because of the sins of the nation, many of which have been highlighted in this book, most especially for our sins of carnality and compromise in the Body of Christ!

I have observed reading through the Bible that whenever Israel was in crisis it was the signal for the nation to come before the Lord and seek His face through prayer and fasting. The question is, can we afford not to do the same?

The people to lead this solemn assembly are the elders of God's people – the Church leaders across all tribes, denominations and streams. These leaders are not only to consecrate themselves and others, they are also to weep between the porch and the altar. These are the days to rend our hearts before God! I really believe this is the heartbeat of God for the Church in this hour. We need to drop our own agendas and ministry commitments and come before God in identificational repentance like Moses, Nehemiah, Ezra, Abraham and other leaders in the Bible.

'Gather the children and nursing babes:
Let the bridegroom go out from his chamber,
And the bride from her dressing room.'

(Joel 2:16, NKJV)

No-one is to be left out of this solemn gathering – not even our children and nursing babes. Not even the bridegroom and his bride! Oh, what a sight that would be! What tremendous effect this can have upon our land and the destiny of the Church. As I write I picture large gatherings, huge football stadiums filled with saints from all over Britain, from every denomination and doctrinal spectrum holding hands, kneeling before God's holy presence crying, weeping and interceding on behalf of the Church and nation!

'Awake . . .
Consecrate a fast,
Call a sacred assembly;
Gather the elders
And all the inhabitants of the land
*Into the house of the L*ORD *your God*
*And cry out to the L*ORD *. . .*
Blow the trumpet in Zion,
And sound an alarm in My holy mountain! . . .
Consecrate a fast,
Call a sacred assembly;
Gather the people,
Sanctify the congregation,
Assemble the elders,
Gather the children and nursing babes;
Let the bridegroom go out from his chamber,
And the bride from her dressing room.
*Let the priests, who minister to the L*ORD*,*
Weep between the porch and the altar;
*Let them say, "Spare Your people, O L*ORD *. . .*
Prepare for war!
Wake up the mighty men.'

(Joel 1:5a; 1:14; 2:1; 2:15–17; 3:9a, NKJV)

Notes

1. Dutch Sheets, *Intercessory Prayer*, Gospel Light (distributed by New Wine Ministries), 1996, p. 240.
2. *Intercessory Prayer*, p. 241.
3. Charles B. Williams, *The New Testament: In the Language of the People*, Chicago, Moody Press, 1937.
4. *Daily Telegraph*, 6 September 2001.
5. *Daily Telegraph*, 26 January 2003.
6. Leonard Ravenhill, *Why Revival Tarries*, Bethany House; 1992 version produced by Sovereign World, Tonbridge, p. 90.
7. *Maranatha News Letter*, Issue 99, November 2003.
8. Leonard Ravenhill, *Why Revival Tarries*, Bethany Books, Minneapolis, 1959.
9. Words by Daniel W. Whittle. 1883, www.cyberhymnal.org
10. New King James Bible, Christian Life Edition, Thomas Nelson, Nashville, 1990, p. 469.
11. *Times Online*, www.timesonline.co.uk
12. Graham Kendrick. Copyright © Kingsway's ThankYou Music, Eastbourne, East Sussex, 1985.
13. Brynmor Pierce Jones, *An Instrument of Revival*, Bridge Logos, 1995, pp. 14–15.
14. Ibid., p. 16.
15. Ibid., p. 189.
16. Colin Whittaker, *Great Revivals*, Marshalls, Basingstoke, 1984, p. 34.
17. Ibid., p. 35.
18. Ibid., p. 41.
19. Ibid., p. 158.
20. Ibid., p. 159.
21. Ibid., p. 159.
22. Ibid., pp. 45–46.
23. Geoff Waugh, *Flashpoints of Revival*, 1998. Rev. Prince J.C. Nwaiwu.
24. Captain E.G. Carre, *Praying Hyde*, Bridge Publishing, 1982, p. 32.
25. Ibid., p. 35.
26. Reinhard Bonnke.
27. Tertullian, 197 AD, Early Church Father, Catholic then Montanist. Lived in Carthage, North Africa.

28. Dr Howard Hendricks, quoted in 'The Importance of a Christian Education', Stanley Jebb, 19 Noweth, Probus, Truro, Cornwall, TR2 9HE, p. 11.

29. Vaughn Shatzer, *History of American Education*, Hearthstone Publishing, Oklahoma 1999, p. 54.

30. Ibid., p. 53.

31. Leonard Ravenhill, *Why Revival Tarries*, Bethany Books, 1959, p. 160.

32. Christian Institute leaflet on sex education. For further information, refer to the video and accompanying resource material *Beyond a Phase: A Practical Guide to Challenging Homophobia in Schools*, Avon Health Promotion Services, 1999.

33. Dr Ted Williams, *Sex Education, Sexual Immorality and the Bible*, Belmont House Publishing, Sutton, Surrey, 2001, p. 2.

34. Ibid., p. 6.

35. Deji Olaopa. Copyright © Deji Olaopa, Ibadan, Nigeria, 1999.

36. Leonard Ravenhill, *Why Revival Tarries*, Bethany Books, 1959, p. 75.

37. Genesis 1:28.

38. M.J. Fisher, *A Topical Study of the Qur'an from a Christian Perspective*, http://answering-islam.org/Authors/Fisher/Topical/. Last updated 1 August 2005.

39. *The Muslim Manifesto: A Strategy for Survival*, p. 16. Produced by The Muslim Institute, 6 Endsleigh Street, London WC1H DD5, 1990.

40. 'Jihad: Struggle, effort. This is the primary meaning of the term as used in the Quran, which refers to an internal effort to reform bad habits in the Islamic community, or within the individual Muslim. The term is also used more specifically to denote a war waged in the service of religion.' Karen Armstrong, *Islam a Short History*, Phoenix Press, London, 2001, p. 170.

41. Source: Al-Muhajiroun publications, *An invitation to Islam*, 11 July 99; their website www.almuhajiroum.com.

42. *Daily Telegraph*, Saturday, 14 December, 1996.

43. Alan Franklin, *EU Final World Empire*, Banner Publishing, Fleet, Hampshire, p. 104.

44. Ibid., p. 104.

45. Ibid., p. 107.

46. *Daily Mail*, 25 September 1987.

47. http://www.amanahfinance.hsbc.com

48. T. Levere, *The Guardian*, Saturday 2 April 2005.

49. *The Times*, Wednesday 10 November, 1993, p. 19.

50. Ibid.

51. *The Times*, Tuesday 9 November, 1993.

52. *The Times*, Tuesday 9 November, 1993, p. 19.

53. *The Times*, 7 January 2002, p. 3.

54. Ibid., p. 2.

55. Ibid., p. 2.

56. Ibid., p. 3.

57. Christian Institute, March 2004 newsletter.
58. *Daily Telegraph*, 10 October 2000.
59. The Christian Institute News Release, Tuesday 30 March 2004.
60. *Daily Telegraph*, 22 June 2002.
61. *Daily Telegraph*, 29 December 2003.
62. *The Times*, 9 April 1999.
63. Christian Peoples Alliance Press Release, 10 January 2005.
64. 'Religious Liberties' – a paper produced by The Christian Institute, p. 12.
65. http://www.advocatesinternational.org
66. *Daily Mail*, 18 October 2001.
67. Islamic Human Rights Commission, Press Release, 7 July 2004.
68. *The Independent*, 8 July 2004.

About World Harvest Christian Centre

World Harvest Christian Centre is a registered charity with its operational base in London, England. We are called by God to spread the message of Jesus Christ and to make people His disciples. We have a calling from God to plant and develop churches and Christian Training Centres in strategic cities of the world.

We inspire and challenge men and women to reach their potential with a deep sense of purpose and destiny. World Harvest Christian Centre incorporates our local fellowship, World Harvest's Missions College, World Harvest Music Academy, World Harvest Christian Nursery and Primary School and World Harvest media.

From our headquarters we endeavour to make the fulfilment of the Great Commission our number one priority. As such, our ministry cuts across racial, denominational, cultural and national lines.

If you would like to visit us, a warm welcome awaits you.

Our service times are:

Sunday
9.00am – 10.30am (1st service) and
10.45am – 12.30pm (2nd service)

Thursday
6.45pm – 9.00pm (Midweek service)

Miracle Breakthrough Service
(*He turned my mourning into dancing*)
First Thursday, Friday and Saturday of every month
Thursday and Friday 7.00pm
Saturday 8.00am

Early Morning Glory
Every Monday to Friday 6.00am–7.00am

To contact World Harvest Christian Centre:

Write to us at:
World Harvest Christian Centre
25–27 Ruby Street (off the Old Kent Road)
London
SE15 1LR

Alternatively:
Email: worldharvestl@aol.com
admin@worldharvest.org.uk

Website: www.worldharvest.org.uk

Telephone: 0207 358 8080

Fax: 0207 358 8088

GREAT BRITAIN HAS FALLEN!

by Wale Babatunde

This first book was published in 2002 highlighting Britain's Christian heritage and should be read alongside *Awake Great Britain!*

Available from:

World Harvest Christian Centre

25–27 Ruby Street, London SE15 1LR

Telephone: 020 7358 8080

or from any Christian bookshop.

ISBN 1-903725-14-3

Cover price: £6.99

THE TRUMPET SOUNDS FOR BRITAIN
by David E. Gardner

David Gardner's central message, in his trilogy *The Trumpet Sounds for Britain*, was to call the people of Great Britain to remember their Christian heritage and turn to the Lord in repentance. Still relevant today, the re-publishing of the book in one volume has made it available as a foundational resource to all who should put the trumpet to their lips.

'David Gardner has provided us with a unique analysis of the Christian heritage of Britain, one that would take an enormous amount of study to repeat.'
(**Dr Clifford Denton** – previous editor of *Prophecy Today*, Christian educationalist preacher and writer. A Cambridge graduate, he received his doctorate at Oxford.)

Available from:
World Harvest Christian Centre
25–27 Ruby Street, London SE15 1LR
Telephone: 020 7358 8080

ISBN 1-903725-20-8
Cover price: £9.99

Special offer
UK orders sent post free to readers of *Awake Great Britain!*.
Please make cheques payable to 'Christian Heritage and Reformation Trust'.

GOD'S ULTIMATUM: To the individual – to the nation – to the whole world

by David E. Gardner

As world history rushes on towards the climax of the ages there is a startling challenge being issued by God from the Bible about the crucial issues which are confronting the nation and the world today.

'*Sometimes a man or woman arises in a nation to give extra emphasis to what an individual, or even the whole nation, needs to hear.*

Such a man was David Gardner; not the only one in his generation to warn the leaders of Britain about the decline from biblical standard and the consequences that would follow of course, but one of the highest calibre nevertheless.'

(**Dr Clifford Denton** – previous editor of *Prophecy Today*, Christian educationalist preacher and writer. A Cambridge graduate, he received his doctorate at Oxford.)

Available from:

World Harvest Christian Centre
25–27 Ruby Street, London SE15 1LR

Telephone: 020 7358 8080

ISBN 1-903725-40-2
Cover price: £7.99

Special offer

UK orders sent post free to readers of *Awake Great Britain!.* Please make cheques payable to 'Christian Heritage and Reformation Trust'.

We hope you enjoyed reading this New Wine book.
For details of other New Wine books
and a range of 2,000 titles from other
Word and Spirit publishers visit our website:
www.newwineministries.co.uk